INSTANT CREATIVITY

SIMPLE TECHNIQUES TO IGNITE
INNOVATION & PROBLEM SOLVING

Brian Clegg and Paul Birch

**KOGAN
PAGE**

London and Philadelphia

Publisher's note
Every possible effort has been made to ensure tht the information contained in this book is accurate at the time of going to press, and the publishers and authors cannot accept responsibility for any errors or omissions, however caused. No responsibility for loss or damage occasioned to any person acting, or refraining from action, as a result of the material in this publication can be accepted by the editor, the publisher or any of the authors.

First published in Great Britain and the United States in 1999 by Kogan Page Limited
This edition 2007

120 Pentonville Road
London N1 9JN
United Kingdom
www.kogan-page.co.uk

525 South 4th Street, #241
Philadelphia PA 19147
USA

© Brian Clegg and Paul Birch, 1999, 2007

The right of Brian Clegg and Paul Birch to be identified as the authors of this work has been asserted by them in accordance with the Copyright, Designs and Patents Act 1988.

ISBN 10 0 7494 4867 9
ISBN 13 978 0 7494 4867 7

British Library Cataloguing-in-Publication Data

A CIP record for this book is available from the British Library.

Library of Congress Cataloguing-in-Publication Data

Clegg, Brian.
    Instant Creativity: simple techniques to ignite innovation and problem solving / Brian Clegg and Paul Birch.
        p. cm
    ISBN 10 0 7494 4867 9
    ISBN 13 978 0 7494 4867 7
1. Creative ability in business—Problems, exercises, etc. 2. exercises, etc. 4. Creative thinking—Problems, exercises, etc. I. Birch, Paul. II. Title.
    HD53.C574 2007
    658.3'14—dc22

                                                                    2006033746

Typeset by Josephine Pierce
Printed and bound in Great Britain by Creative Print and Design (Wales), Ebbw Vale

Contents

Why creativity?

Creativity or bust

Depending on your point of view, the prospects for business are terrifying or elating. Once upon a time, business life was a bit like being on a train, moving from station to station according to a timetable. Now it's a roller coaster that has lost its guard rails. There has never been more pressure. Competitive pressures as more new ideas, more new competitors hit the market. Cost pressures as customers demand more for less. Customer service pressures as those pesky customers expect good service on top of all the savings. Time pressures as blossoming technology compresses everything from communications to the manufacturing cycle into less and less time.

There's only one way out. Creativity. It's not fanciful to state that without creativity there are very few companies in existence today that will still be around in a few years' time. Change is the name of the game, and innovation is what is needed to stay above water as yet another wave of change hits the shore. Without creativity you are going to be wheeling out the same old solutions to problems. Sorry, won't work – the problems are changing under your feet, and the opposition is getting better all the time. And you'll be pushing the same old products and services. Sorry again. They're already out of date. Creativity isn't a nice-to-have, it's a survival factor.

Can you catch it from a book?

It is all very well to acknowledge that every business needs creativity, but it's quite a different prospect to do something about it. A natural inclination might be to rush out and recruit some creative people. That may not be a bad idea. But the fact is that everyone has a lot more creativity in them than they generally use.

There are a number of reasons for this. It might be the wrong time of day. Your participants may be tired, stressed or bored. And worst of all, everyone's natural potential for creativity has been suppressed. This comes from a combination of socialization – it is often advisable to lower creativity to enhance survival prospects – and education, which is generally more about getting to the required answer than coming up with a creative solution. There is nothing wrong with this, but it gets in the way when you need creativity.

This book can't inject a magic dose of creativity from a big syringe labelled 'innovation', but it can act as a catalyst to free up some of the natural creativity that is bottled up by habit, training and (lack of) energy. The bulk of the book consists of a series of short exercises and techniques, designed to shatter constraints and to get the participants thinking differently. These techniques aren't creative in themselves, any more than a typewriter or PC actually produces novels. But they are effective tools to release our pent-up creativity.

What's the hurry?

An essential aspect of this book is the 'instant' in the title. These aren't lengthy, long-winded processes to establish an innovation framework (or other such management gobbledegook), but quick hits to push up the creativity level. Such an approach isn't always beneficial. In Chapter 6, you will find references to a number of books that will help with larger scale creativity initiatives. These more structured approaches are absolutely essential when dealing with a large problem, or looking to implement systematic creativity in a company. We would very much recommend that you investigated these, too. They will help to transform your company. But there is often the need for urgency.

Think how often you have had to come up with a solution to a problem quickly. Or there was only time for 10 minutes of the meeting to be dedicated to it. Or there was immense pressure to get something done. Or you had to come up with some fresh ideas by yesterday. The fact is, the need for creativity goes hand-in-hand with time pressure. Without instant creativity in your tool bag to complement any longer term approaches, the chances are you will never get off the ground.

Creativity primer

What is it?

It is possible to know you really need something without being sure what it is – creativity is a bit like that. The problem with creativity is that it's a blanket term for several related things. There's artistic creativity – the production of a book or painting or piece of music – that is in some way original. There's the creativity of discovery, whether it's Archimedes leaping out of his bath shouting 'Eureka!' or a new product concept. And there's the creativity of humour. There is something special about humour, because it involves seeing the world in a different way, and that is an essential for creativity.

It is true that much business creativity revolves around the second of those types. We are looking for the solution to a business problem, or an idea to come up with a new product or service. Yet in reality, almost every act of creativity merges the three. To be really innovative, the chances are there will be elements of artistic creativity present – whether it's in the elegance of a business plan or the style of a design. And to be creative effectively usually demands the presence of humour. If this is a problem, ask yourself what you've got against people enjoying themselves, just because they're working. Does it really make sense?

What stops it?

It is often easier to stop people being creative than to enhance their creativity. We do it all the time. We have already referred to the restraints of social and educational conditioning. It's not surprising that there are social restraints on creativity. Young children have a very creative view of the world. They aren't constrained by habit and teaching. But they are also at risk from hazards they aren't prepared for. Some of our creativity is pushed aside to keep us safe. Yet when using creativity to solve a business problem we are in a safe, cushioned environment. We can afford to take more virtual risks; in fact we need to if something new and wonderful is to emerge.

In education creativity is frowned upon because it runs counter to the desired output. Like it or not, our education system is largely designed to get young people through exams. This means getting them to give the answers the examiners want. Not the most original answer, not the creative answer, but the single right answer that is on the answer sheet. Real life isn't like that. Any problem, any requirement is likely to have many right answers. When we need to get creative it is because the obvious answer isn't good enough. Someone else has already done it. It has already been tried. We need something new and different.

If being creative means taking risks, appearing silly (most great ideas sound crazy initially) and failing more frequently, we've another problem. These traits are not popular. As individuals, we don't like them. Corporate culture is generally very heavy on failure. 'You only get one chance to make a mistake here.' Even very constructive measures like total quality management (TQM) have their downside, because the implication is that failure is always bad. Yet there's only one way to be really original. To throw off restraint, and go for it. There will be lots of failure, but it shouldn't matter because failure is the best basis for learning – and it is only by sticking your neck out that you will also achieve real creativity. One of the best ways to improve creativity quickly is to prevent the fresh green shoots of new ideas from being trampled on by practicality. Until everyone is prepared to come up with something they think will sound silly, knowing it won't be laughed at or frowned on, you won't have a truly creative team.

As if that isn't enough, there is yet another danger. The expert syndrome. We are increasingly developing a culture of experts. Expertise is one of the prime commodities we have to sell. Yet expertise can be dangerous when it comes to creativity. Expertise depends on knowing a lot about how things have been before. While the best experts can then flexibly interpret a different situation, all too often expertise means tunnel vision when faced with the new. We should be looking for creative input beyond those who are very closely involved in a project or business if we want real innovation. Don't throw your experts away, but take your input more widely.

Why techniques?

The main enemies of creativity are tunnel vision and lack of inspiration. Either we know too much about the past to do anything but continue trudging down the same path, or we haven't got the vision to see a new destination. The idea of a creativity technique – of pretty well all the techniques in Chapters 4 and 5   is to push you away from that well-trodden path. To get a different viewpoint, by forcing you to do something you wouldn't normally do. This can be uncomfortable, but it is the only way to make something happen.

This explains why something as mechanical and often irrelevant seeming as a technique can have such stunning results. Creativity techniques aren't creative; you are. What they are superb at, though, is pushing you to a different starting point, providing you with an opportunity to make new associations, helping you to take a fresh view and come up with something completely different.

Associations to ideas

Many of the techniques we describe require you to make associations with something and then relate these associations back to the problem or requirement. Rather than take up space within each of the techniques to explain this process we have tried to give an overview here that will serve for all of them.

In some ways this is the hardest part of the creativity process, although even this isn't as hard as some would have you believe. This is the point where you take a mechanical technique and apply genuine creativity to it. This aspect of the process is highly dependent on experience. The more you do it, the easier it will become. Because of this, we strongly advise regular practice using the exercises in this book, even if you don't have a specific problem to solve. This is particularly important when you are new to the field of creativity.

Let us assume that you are trying to develop a new confectionery product and that you have used a creativity technique that has generated the following associations:

whiskers, collar, fur, fleas, paws, hunter, after dark, mice, killer, cuddly, fun, warm, friendly, aloof, independent, lazy, active, angry, spitting, hissing, claws, teeth

In case it isn't obvious, we used the *Random word* technique (5.7) with the word *cat*.

With product development, more than with most problem solving or idea generation, you have the option of inserting an intermediate phrase into the translation process from the association to the idea. This is to describe your non-existent product in terms of the association. In this case we are looking for 'The <something> confectionery' or 'The confectionery with <something>'. For instance:

The cuddly confectionery
The killer confectionery
The furry confectionery

The confectionery with whiskers
The active confectionery

Sometimes, when reading such a list, immediate ideas will pop into your mind as to what this phrase might mean. The second stage is to write a more detailed description of this. For instance, 'The confectionery with whiskers' rather oddly made us think of old-aged confectionery. This made us think of more mature confectionery. We saw this going in two directions, either confectionery for the more mature palette or confectionery that is matured for a fuller flavour.

On reading that through, you may have seen some ideas of your own. You may have thought that the ideas we have generated are not all that great. That doesn't really matter. What matters is that the process is clear. This two-stage process can be used wherever you can describe the problem in terms of a sentence in which you can insert a range of words.

Where this is not the case, you must move more directly from the association words to ideas. To show an example of this let's assume that we have the same words as above, but that we are trying to solve the problem of poor attendance in a factory. This is harder to create sentences for so we must move more directly.

Looking at the list, 'killer' made us think of killing off poor attendees. Not immediately practical, but this could be developed as an idea where an attendance monitoring scheme is implemented that ultimately results in the dismissal of those with poor attendance records. 'Collar' made us think of control and this led to the idea of high levels of follow-up and checking of attendance problems – talking to everyone after they have missed a day and finding out why, insisting on doctors' notes, etc. 'Fun' made us think of making the workplace more fun so that people don't feel the need to stay away. 'Independent' made us think of making small groups of staff responsible for their own results regardless of attendance. You can see how this works. These ideas are half-baked. This is always true at this stage of the process. Treat them like tender green shoots that need love and attention. If you trample on them too early in their lives (by evaluating them), you will kill them.

The longer view

We emphasized the need for the 'instant' approach in the first chapter. However, to get the most out of creativity you will need to take a longer view, too. If (or rather, when) the techniques in this book prove effective, consider the opportunities for making more of creativity. See Chapter 6 for suggestions on reading, information technology and more to widen your creative armoury.

The techniques

Questions and answers

This book is not designed to be read from beginning to end, but to be dipped into as a resource. The techniques in *Instant Creativity* are split into two sections: 'What's the question?' (Chapter 4) and 'What's the answer?' (Chapter 5). This division corresponds to two very different parts of the creative process. Sometimes you will need to use one, sometimes the other, sometimes both.

'What's the question?' is about discovering what your problem is. This might seem unnecessary. Surely you already know what the problem is? You want to decrease packaging costs by 10 per cent. Or you want to get into the European market. Or you want to come up with a new product in your range. Or whatever.

The trouble is, we aren't always clear what it is that we need. It could be that the requirement is rather vague. We want to increase profits, but it isn't clear in what area, or why. It could be that the initial assessment of the problem is dealing with a symptom, not a cause. Let's say the problem was originally thought to be 'how to improve staff timekeeping', and it turned out that people were coming in late because there were always traffic jams on the access road. Then a more effective problem to attack might be 'how to get the staff to work without being stuck in a traffic jam'.

Whatever the consideration, the outcome of the 'what's the question' exercises is to determine an appropriate statement of your requirement. This is usually best phrased in a pithy statement beginning 'how to'. When you have such a statement – and that may already be the case – in comes the second set of techniques, 'What's the answer?'. These are specifically designed to break down the walls of your tunnel vision and to give you a new viewpoint, to enable you to come up with fresh ideas.

The final few techniques (from 5.50 onwards) are a special case of the 'what's the answer' type. Instead of being designed for developing a solution, they are about choosing an idea from a number that have been generated, and refining it. Whichever technique you use, you may need one of these extras to fine-tune your output.

Individuals and groups

Practically all the techniques in this book can be used both individually and with groups. Creativity is a compound process. The initial generation of ideas is often best done as an individual activity, but the development, combination and refinement of those ideas works better with a group. Where possible, we will suggest ways of working partly as individuals and partly as groups, but don't let the constraints of your resources get in the way – you can always be creative

Choosing a technique

Some techniques are better than others for different types of application. Apart from the split between techniques to generate questions and techniques to generate answers, we offer a number of other options in the ratings given to each technique. In Appendix 1 you will find a range of tables from which to select a technique based on a particular requirement. There is also a random technique selector. This gives access to the more generally applicable techniques, allowing one to be selected instantly. This can often be beneficial. If you habitually use one or other technique, that approach itself can get you into a rut. Random selection can help break out.

The *Instant Creativity* structure

Each technique is presented in a standard format, with brief details of any preparation required, running time, resources used and team applicability, followed by a description of the technique itself. This is followed by suggestions for feedback, comments on the outcome and possible variations on the technique. The final part of the entry is the rating. As much as possible, to keep with the 'instant' theme, the techniques require minimal preparation, but some techniques requiring a little more work beforehand are included as they can sometimes be particularly effective. Note that timings are for minimum time – you can take longer over most of the techniques if it is appropriate.

Techniques 1

What's the question?

These techniques are particularly appropriate for the early stages of a process. The two key requirements here are to get a better understanding of just what the problem is, and to come up with a general direction for attack.

4.1 Compass

Preparation:	A basic statement of your problem or requirement.
Running time:	Five minutes.
Resources:	None.
Teams:	Individual/team.

The *Compass* is a direction setting technique that is used to find the real problems that underlie the problem statement as presented. In order to make it work, you need to have developed a problem statement, ideally one that is owned by somebody within the group – try to put it in the form 'how to…'. You then merely ask 'why' a great deal.

Given the initial problem statement ask 'why'. In other words, 'why is this a problem?' or, 'why do you see it like that?' Whatever is the answer to this question, write it down and then probe the answer itself by asking 'why' again. Repeat this process on the next answer. This continues until you feel you have hit a dead end or until it all becomes terminally dull. For instance, if my problem is how to write this book faster. Why? Because I don't want to spend so much time on it. Why? Because I want to spend more time with my family. This can continue for some time from here.

You will find that each response to each question can be rephrased to form a 'how to' problem statement. Some of these will be much more fruitful areas of exploration than the original problem.

Feedback

It sounds simple and it is. That is not to say that it isn't useful. We've seen a problem entirely solved by merely rephrasing the problem statement, so don't underestimate the benefit of spending time doing this.

Outcome

This is a very effective way of getting new questions and new directions from which to tackle a problem. You will find that the more you use this technique, the better you get at asking subtly different why questions that don't sound so repetitive.

Variations

This activity can be run as a full group session or as a number of team sessions.

Expertise: ✓
Direction setting: ✓✓✓✓
Idea generation: ✓
Problem solving: ✓
Fun: ✓✓

4.2 Obstacle map

Preparation:	None.
Running time:	Five minutes.
Resources:	Flip charts (ideally three).
Teams:	Individual/team.

Line up three flip chart stands, or stick three sheets of flip chart paper on the wall. Start by outlining your objective. In pithy phrases, describe what you want to achieve and what things will be like when you succeed. If you are dealing with a product, this might be product characteristics or customer benefits. If you are dealing with a problem, it could be a world where the problem no longer exists. This output should be written on the far right flip chart.

Next, on the far left chart, describe the current state. Using the same factors as the description of your objective, where are you now? What is the world like?

In between, list the obstacles to achieving your outcome. Some obstacles may be reiterations or restatements of the starting position – this isn't a problem, your starting position often is an obstacle in its own right.

Most of the obstacles you have listed can now be rephrased as 'how to' statements. These form alternative problem statements, expanding your understanding of the question you are trying to answer.

Feedback

Resist the temptation to jump straight to the obstacles. It is difficult to hold all the considerations in your head at once. Putting them on paper frees you to think of one thing at a time and improves the results significantly. Also, in a group some will have different views of where you are going or even where you are starting. It is important to capture these.

Outcome

You are likely to find that you generate more 'how to' statements than you can use. Very often in the creative process you will generate more than you need and only use some of it. This is not a problem, it is the nature of the beast.

Variations

The ways that you write up the *Obstacle map* can be varied immensely. Try giving each group member sticky notes, or getting each group member to work independently first. However, don't be tempted to avoid writing all three parts down.

Expertise:	✓
Direction setting:	✓✓✓✓
Idea generation:	✓
Problem solving:	✓
Fun:	✓

4.3 The level chain

Preparation:	None.
Running time:	Five minutes.
Resources:	None.
Teams:	Individual.

The *Level chain* works by taking a random chain of items, products, concepts – whatever fits the requirement – and using it to generate fresh ideas. Start with something to do with the area you are looking at for a new idea – or something completely different. Then generate a chain of objects or concepts that are either more general (at a higher level), or more specific (at a lower level). Whenever your chain makes you think of an idea, stop and note it down. For example, a chain looking for a new telecoms product, starting at phone, might go (up to) communicator (down to) politician (down to) bench (up to) seating. Now an idea strikes. Why not have an armchair with a built-in phone, so you can chat comfortably?

It is important that the participants don't analyse during the *Level chain*. Let the chain flow in almost free association, stopping whenever something attracts your attention. Chains should be quick – in five minutes it should be possible to generate 5 to 10 chains.

Feedback

The *Level chain* is very easy to pick up once it has been demonstrated, but it is essential to have an example. If pulling together the output from a number of individuals, it is best to get some verbal feedback on where their chains went, but only note down the outcomes.

Outcome

This is a superb vehicle for generating new ideas, products and services. It almost invariably comes up with a good range of original possibilities, and is a good exercise to persuade participants of the value of creativity techniques.

Variations

The *Level chain* is essentially individual, but can be stretched in various ways. Used in a group, it is best if each person conducts their own chains, then shares the outcome. An alternative approach, which works particularly well using e-mail, is for one individual to start a chain, then send it around a distribution list, with each recipient adding one item to the chain.

Expertise:	✓✓
Direction setting:	✓✓✓
Idea generation:	✓✓✓
Problem solving:	✓
Fun:	✓✓✓

4.4 Aerial survey

Preparation:	None.
Running time:	10 minutes.
Resources:	Paper, flip chart or whiteboard and pens.
Teams:	Individual/team.

Aerial survey is a technique aimed at giving an overview of your problem area and therefore additional insights into your problem. It involves drawing a mind map of the available information.

The mind mapping technique, developed by Tony Buzan, is quite simple in concept. You start at the centre of a page, or whiteboard, and draw an image that represents the core of the issue. From this, you radiate out branches that represent the major themes of the issue. From each of these, you draw progressively lower and lower level themes.

On each of the branches, write one or two keywords above the line to say what that issue is. For instance, one branch might be profit – splitting into costs and revenues – with revenues splitting into direct sales and indirect and costs splitting into the major cost drivers. In general, try to make the image organic. Start with larger and fatter branches at the centre, moving to smaller and smaller ones and eventually twigs at the extremities. You might also use different colours for each major branch (and make all subsidiaries the same colour as the major branch).

Feedback

Don't get too hung up on the process of drawing the aerial survey. Remember that the overall objective is an image-based overview of the problem and not to produce a work of art.

Outcome

This technique does not directly generate additional 'how to' statements, but does give a very good overview of the problem, pulling out aspects that might otherwise have been overlooked, and so helps to create a direction.

Variations

There are many different ways to draw mind maps. For more information, see Tony and Barry Buzan's *The Mind Map Book* (details in Chapter 6). While described as an individual activity, *Aerial survey* can work well with a group as a way of achieving consensus on the issues faced. If the group needs some creative stimulation, give them paints, crayons and chalks and tell them to make the mind map attractive as well as informative.

Expertise: ✓✓✓
Direction setting: ✓✓✓✓
Idea generation: ✓
Problem solving: ✓
Fun: ✓

4.5 Destination

Preparation:	None.
Running time:	Five minutes.
Resources:	None.
Teams:	Individual/team.

The best representation of a problem (or requirement for an idea) is usually a statement beginning 'how to…'. This statement is akin to a destination in a journey. It is your point B when travelling from A to B. Often the issue that you face is that you cannot see a way to get there, but you are sure that B is where you want to get to. This technique is an opportunity to question this position.

Really, technique is too strong a word. *Destination* is merely the act of questioning whether you really need to achieve your 'how to', or whether another destination would be as good or better.

Some of the techniques in this book produce different 'how to' statements. If you have time you can work on a selection of these. Whether you do this or not, consider any alternative formulations of the problem that spring to mind. There is always a temptation to hang on to your initial statement because that's the 'real' one.

Take a moment to display the range of 'how to' statements in front of you. Is there one statement that better encapsulates the whole problem than the one you started with? If so, switch to it. If not, stay with the original.

Feedback

The reason that we have listed this as a technique is that it is a crucial stage in the creativity process and one that is too easily overlooked. The work that you invest in developing alternative views of your problem is devalued if you always regard your original statement as the real problem and the others as subsidiary.

Outcome

In our experience, you will decide to drop your original problem statement about half of the time.

Variations

You can select an alternative statement by discussion, but there may still be argument. If it proves difficult, try using one of the selection techniques (beginning with number 5.50) in the next section.

Expertise: ✓
Direction setting: ✓✓✓
Idea generation: ✓
Problem solving: ✓
Fun: ✓

4.6 Do nothing

Preparation:	None.
Running time:	Five minutes.
Resources:	None.
Teams:	Individual/team.

What would happen if you did nothing?

The difficulty with taking this stance is that it is very easy to become wedded to the idea that we must do something, anything. This leads us to regard the 'do nothing' option as completely unacceptable. This, in turn, leads us to create exaggerated claims of the difficulties that we will face if we do nothing.

Stop and think for a while. If you are in a group, take a moment to discuss it. What would really happen if you were to do nothing?

Assuming that you decide that your problem still needs to be solved, this process leads to two outcomes. Firstly, you will have a better idea of the benefits that will accrue from solving the problem. Secondly, you will have generated some alternative problems to solve by discussing the difficulties that would arise as a result of doing nothing. For instance, let us assume that the problem was that a product line had to become more profitable next year than it had in the past, and the 'do nothing' discussion had highlighted the reason as being a tax break coming to an end. An alternative problem would be to extend or replace the tax break.

Feedback

If you use none of the other techniques for questioning your 'how to' statement you should use this one.

Outcome

You will end up with a better understanding of your 'how to' statement and you will possibly have generated some alternatives. You may even end up deciding to do nothing – this really does happen. This may generate a new problem – persuading the problem owner to give it up. *Do nothing* can also generate new solutions to problems – not doing nothing itself, but arising out of the consequences of doing nothing.

Variations

As well as conducting this as an individual exercise, or as a group discussion, you could conduct a discussion by e-mail, fax or letter. Lay out for all interested parties your understanding of the problem and have them respond with their analysis of the result of doing nothing.

> **Expertise:** ✓
> **Direction setting:** ✓✓✓✓
> **Idea generation:** ✓
> **Problem solving:** ✓✓✓
> **Fun:** ✓✓

4.7 **Shorts**

Preparation:	None.
Running time:	5 to 10 minutes.
Resources:	Book of short stories.
Teams:	Individual.

In principle, this is a ridiculously simple exercise. Take a book of short stories. Take a minute to think through your problem area first. Then read a story you have never read before. As you do so, don't make a conscious effort to bring your problem area to mind – your awareness of undertaking this exercise as a technique will make sure that the problem remains active in your subconscious.

When you have read the story, come back to the problem area. Revisit the requirements. You needn't make heavy-handed links with the story, but anything it made you think of can be employed. In surprisingly many cases, you will find new possibilities opening up.

Feedback

This technique suffers from a traditional business hang-up: you aren't supposed to enjoy yourself at work. Because of this, it may be as hard to justify using this technique to yourself as it is to justify it to your business colleagues. If you have difficulties, try it first at lunchtime or some other recognized break. But be aware that your action makes the technique less effective. It implies that you don't really believe in the benefits of what you are doing. This will not have a positive effect.

Outcome

This technique can be used to develop solutions too, but the general nature of the approach is particularly suited to formulating the questions. Don't be put off if there's no real benefit the first time. Try it on a few occasions before giving it up. For some people, this approach simply doesn't work, but for many it is effective.

Variations

A short story is particularly suited to this approach, although other types of fiction, and even dramatic non-fiction, can work. Be prepared to step outside your habitual reading areas. Probably the best source is science fiction (which also has more short stories than most genres). Romantic fiction is less productive, but adventure and crime can be effective. If you don't know any science fiction, the Creativity Unleashed bookshop can help. See the *Reading up* section in Chapter 6.

Expertise: ✓✓
Direction setting: ✓✓✓
Idea generation: ✓✓
Problem solving: ✓✓
Fun: ✓✓✓

4.8 Adventure

Preparation:	None.
Running time:	10 minutes to one hour.
Resources:	PC, computer game.
Teams:	Individual.

Run a computer game on your PC. While the program starts up, take a minute to think through your problem area. Then spend a short time playing the game. As you do so, don't make a conscious effort to bring your problem area to mind.

After a few minutes, save your position (so next time you use the game you will start at a different point). Now, revisit the requirements. You needn't make heavy-handed links with the game, but anything it made you think of can be employed. In surprisingly many cases, you will find new possibilities opening up.

Feedback

If reading fiction in working time (*Shorts*, 4.7) is frowned upon, playing a game is even worse. A first attempt at this technique is probably best undertaken in a neutral environment. If it works for you, it can be introduced into the workplace. In principle this technique can be performed as quickly as any other, but the difficulty of playing a game for a few minutes without getting engrossed may make it take longer.

Outcome

This technique can be used to generate problem solutions too, but it is particularly suited to formulating the questions. Don't be put off if there is no real benefit the first time. Try it on a few occasions before giving it up. For some people, this approach simply doesn't work, but for many it is effective. The active nature of the game will help to stimulate new connections and possibilities.

Variations

Computer games are not everyone's cup of tea. As there is more personal effort involved, it is probably best restricted to those who are comfortable with the format. The best games for this technique are those which don't involve heavy duty puzzle solving or complex repetition. Instead, an 'interactive movie' which leads the player through much of the action is better. Given that the intent is to gain creative stimulation rather than good gameplay, consider downloading a 'walk-through' from the internet to help with frustrating hold-ups.

Expertise:	✓✓
Direction setting:	✓✓✓
Idea generation:	✓✓
Problem solving:	✓✓
Fun:	✓✓✓✓

4.9 Outside in

Preparation:	None.
Running time:	10 minutes.
Resources:	None.
Teams:	Individual.

A real difficulty when attempting to clarify a problem is the impact of your working environment. This technique is probably the easiest in this book. Take a quick glance over the information you have already assessed about your problem, then go outside. It doesn't matter if you work in the heart of the country or on an industrial estate – spend five minutes walking about, taking in the sights, sounds and smells around you.

When you return to the office, revisit your problem area. Does anything seem different immediately? Is there anything you experienced on your excursion that might make the requirement different? Use what you have seen, heard and smelled as resource.

Feedback

While there is much debate about the nature of knowledge, it is widely agreed that most of our understanding of the world is stored in the form of mental pictures, using metaphors and associations that derive from the primary senses, like sight and sound. Because of this, a conscious effort to experience the world away from your working environment, paying more attention to the senses than is normal, can be a very constructive stimulus.

Outcome

This approach can be used as a variant on *Found objects* (5.9) when looking for solutions, but it is particularly suited to finding the right questions, because the broad nature of the stimulus is more tuned to setting directions than coming up with specific solutions.

Variations

It is quite enough simply to go outside and take in what is around you to be able to generate new ideas. The creative process is also helped by the move to fresh air and different temperatures. To make the technique better suited to idea generation or problem solving, fix on the particular sight, smell or sound which most interests you. Note down what is special about it. When you return to the office, use the same approach as *Found objects* on your specific experience. Some people find driving a car a particularly effective 'outside', as the semi-automatic nature of the task seems to stimulate thought.

Expertise: ✓
Direction setting: ✓✓✓
Idea generation: ✓✓
Problem solving: ✓✓
Fun: ✓✓

4.10 Up and down

Preparation: None.
Running time: 10 minutes.
Resources: None.
Teams: Individual/team.

When formulating the problem, it is natural to take your own point of view. In this exercise, you will spend a few minutes looking up and down from your position. If you are at the very top of the company, try looking to the middle, then even further down to the bottom.

First look up. Put yourself in the position of the chief executive. What would he or she see as the underlying problem, the obstacle to success, or the new product direction? Try directly formulating the question from their viewpoint, then spend a minute thinking through the influences and requirements of this particular person, and try again. Then look down. What would the lowliest worker in the company see as the problem? How would they see the problem affecting them and their world? Use these two insights to formulate different 'how to' statements.

Feedback

Looking in these diverging directions can produce very different views of the problem. Try to think like real people, not caricatures. The top person isn't just concerned about company profitability (although this is important). The lowly worker isn't just worried about wage packets and working conditions. Take a broader view.

Outcome

This technique can be used as a variant on *Someone else's view* (5.5) when looking for solutions, but it is particularly suited to finding the right questions, because these different views are just as important as your own when coming to a picture of the desired direction. The very different circumstances and needs underlying the viewpoints will combine to produce a much rounder, fuller picture of the problem.

Variations

It is possible to talk to the real people involved, but the person at the top may not have time, and the person at the bottom may find it difficult to give you the required information. Try splitting a team in two. Each half takes one of the standpoints, spending a few minutes developing their ideas. Then let them share the ideas in a mock meeting, being prepared, if necessary, to stand up for their position and knock down anything that seems unreasonable.

Expertise:	✓✓
Direction setting:	✓✓✓✓
Idea generation:	✓✓
Problem solving:	✓✓
Fun:	✓✓

4.11 Time slices

Preparation:	None.
Running time:	10 minutes.
Resources:	None.
Teams:	Individual/team.

Look at your problem area. Consider each of the following timescales: one minute, one day, one week, one month, one year. What is critical in each of these timescales? How will the problem change? What has to be considered in the different timings? What influences come into play? Would you state the problem differently if each of these timings was an imposed deadline (for completion of the entire requirement)? Would the 'how to' statement come out differently? If there isn't an imposed deadline, what considerations are likely to impact your problem on these timescales?

Feedback

It is easy to make assumptions about timings that may not be valid, or at least may not be necessary. This technique forces you to examine your timing assumptions and how they impact the direction you are likely to take. The deadlines may not really be imposed, but trying out the assumptions of those deadlines can result in a considerable improvement in understanding. Often the significant 80 per cent solution is achieved in a fraction of the overall time, while the remaining time is spent on fining up the last details. Sometimes (for example, when looking at nuclear power plant safety), those details are critical – often they are irrelevant.

Outcome

This technique will not produce solutions, or even precise 'how to' statements. Instead, it produces a better broad understanding of just what the problem area is, which is essential (particularly with a complex problem) to coming to a sensible statement of the problem and a practical, creative solution.

Variations

You may need to modify the timescales considered to fit a problem where there is already a reasonably clear end point in time, even if the destination is not clear. Make sure, though, that there are several very different timescales involved. A group can split up and take one timescale per team – this reduces the monotony of repetition and makes a debate on the importance of different timescales a more effective contributor to the process.

Expertise:	✓✓
Direction setting:	✓✓✓
Idea generation:	✓
Problem solving:	✓✓
Fun:	✓✓

4.12 Thesaurus

Preparation:	Basic 'how to' statement.
Running time:	Five minutes.
Resources:	Access to an online or book thesaurus.
Teams:	Individual/team.

If you need to find an alternative word when you are writing, you turn to the thesaurus. It offers different perspectives on meaning. In many ways, that's exactly what you are trying to do when you are setting a direction. You are looking for different perspectives on a given requirement. So, why not use a thesaurus as a kick-start to the idea generation process?

Start with a problem statement in the form of 'how to...'. You won't be sure of your direction yet, but take a stab at it. Then identify the key words from that statement and use a thesaurus to find alternatives. Find a few that are fundamentally different to the starting position.

Now use these words as stimuli, either for rephrasing the problem statement or for coming up with a whole new direction to take.

Feedback

One of the reasons why this technique seems to work well is that it doesn't feel as though you are throwing away the initial problem statement as some other techniques might. One of the tough things to explain about the creative process is the need to move right away from the problem in order to kick the mind into a different way of thinking. This technique does that, but still feels as though you are connected back to the problem.

Outcome

Thesaurus works well as a way of generating alternative perspectives on the problem but it is also very effective at generating new associations and, from there, brand new ideas.

Variations

In using this technique we have used a paper-based thesaurus, a computer one and a pocket electronic thesaurus. In some ways the pocket one worked best because it allowed you to scroll through alternative meanings one at a time and so it was harder to skim over and ignore one.

Expertise:	✓✓
Direction setting:	✓✓✓
Idea generation:	✓✓✓
Problem solving:	✓✓
Fun:	✓✓

4.13 Crystal ball

Preparation:	None.
Running time:	10 minutes.
Resources:	None.
Teams:	Individual/team.

Consider three different scenarios and make totally different key assumptions about your problem. Inevitably there will be some unknowns – there will be outside influences and changes ahead that you can't predict. Go in for some serious speculation. What if... the stock market collapsed, war broke out, your main competitor went bust or was bought out by a much bigger company. The possibilities are endless – just choose three that appeal to you and are very different from each other.

For each scenario, generate two new 'how to' statements, assuming the scenario were true. Now take these 'how to' statements and give them a mild dose of reality. The 'how to' statements will give you a better understanding of the problem area however extreme they are, but you may need to make minor modifications before adopting one as the actual problem statement.

Feedback

We all make assumptions when deciding what the problem is, but creativity is all about challenging assumptions. By forcing yourself to take several very different scenarios as your starting point you are more likely to see beyond the obvious aspects of the problem, uncovering facets which would otherwise have remained hidden. You may stick with your original assumptions, but trying out alternatives is educational.

Outcome

Often an alternative will not have been examined because the outcome is too frightening. By forcing yourself to consider alternative scenarios, you will come up with a much wider range of 'how to's and may also uncover some unpleasant truths.

Variations

You may need to try more than three scenarios if the problem is complex. Try to identify the key dimensions of the problem area and vary these dimensions. Groups will find it more constructive to assign one scenario to each of a number of smaller teams.

Expertise:	✓✓
Direction setting:	✓✓✓
Idea generation:	✓
Problem solving:	✓
Fun:	✓✓

4.14 Web wandering

Preparation:	Basic 'how to' statement.
Running time:	10 minutes.
Resources:	Computer with internet connection.
Teams:	Individual / team.

Formulate a first shot 'how to' statement for your problem. Don't put a lot of effort into this – just let it flow. Now identify the key words in the statement. There will typically be two to five of these – the words that carry the real significance of the problem.

Use an internet search engine such as Google (**http://www. google.co.uk**). Enter the keywords into the search box. Now spend five minutes browsing the results. As you do, consider your 'how to' statement. How might it be modified, bearing in mind the associations generated by the pages you are looking at? What new options and possibilities arise from what you see?

Feedback

To use this technique effectively, you need to have developed a reasonable skill at making associations. If this doesn't feel natural, check out page 8 in Chapter 2 for a quick primer. Note that this is quite a different use of the internet as a resource to that in *Cool site* (5.12). There the web page is used as a random stimulus to generate ideas and solutions. Here it is exploring different aspects of the question using direct associations.

Outcome

This approach is a very good one if you have a starting version of your question, but would like to explore alternatives and make sure that you are answering the right question. The breadth of information on the web will inevitably generate some very different aspects of your direction.

Variations

Try putting the keywords in separately or together. If several computers are available, let each team take a different search engine, rather than a different keyword, as the results can be very different. If possible, use both UK and US engines.

Expertise:	✓✓✓
Direction setting:	✓✓✓✓
Idea generation:	✓✓
Problem solving:	✓
Fun:	✓✓✓

4.15 **Excellence**

Preparation:	Basic 'how to' statement.
Running time:	Five minutes.
Resources:	None.
Teams:	Individual/team.

Formulate a first shot 'how to' statement for your problem. Don't put a lot of effort into this – just let it flow. Most 'how to' statements are initially quite restrained. The object of this exercise is to push them into excellence.

Whatever the nature of your statement, make it more extreme. For example, if you said 'how to increase productivity', make it 'how to have the best productivity in our industry'. If you said 'increase sales by 10 per cent', make it 'increase sales by 100 per cent'. Look for excellence in your statement. However high the aspirations of your rough 'how to' statement, make them even higher.

Now consider the implications. It may be enough to say that the extreme 'how to' should be your goal. Often excellence is both desirable and achievable. In some cases, though, you might have made a 'how to' statement that is either impractical or undesirable. For example, you might have gone from 'how to dominate our market' to 'how to dominate the world'. In such a case, consider how you might modify your original statement to make it more like the extreme – have more of the qualities of the extreme – without the negative or impossible aspects.

Feedback

This is a technique that shouldn't be used too often. Most particularly, don't think of using this technique when you originally come up with your rough 'how to' statement. If you have already decided to use it, make sure it isn't part of your original formulation. Don't be tempted to come up with an extreme statement initially. Start with an eminently practical statement, then push for excellence.

Outcome

A major reason for employing creativity techniques is to go beyond the ordinary to the extraordinary. This technique ensures that your goal is not too mundane, too easily achievable. It is very effective at tuning up a direction to your best advantage.

Variations

There are no significant variations. If you aren't getting much result, try a second iteration – push your excellence statement to even greater extremes and consider the consequences.

Expertise:	✓✓
Direction setting:	✓✓✓✓
Idea generation:	✓
Problem solving:	✓
Fun:	✓✓

4.16 Army of a thousand

Preparation:	None.
Running time:	Five minutes.
Resources:	None.
Teams:	Individual/team.

You have a thousand people at your disposal. They can have any expertise you like. You set them to work on solving your problem. What would they do? How would they devise a solution? What can you learn from this?

Now you have the same army to implement a solution. How would you achieve it with this dedicated, cost-free army? What would be needed? Use the outcome of these two exercises to feed into your actual solution.

Feedback

You (probably) won't have a huge, cost-free army who are desperate to do your bidding in practice. Don't worry about this. Any ideas that are generated will need to be modified to fit your actual resources. But the direction may well be a new one that you wouldn't otherwise have considered, because the real resources at your disposal will have limited your vision. This technique dates back to our early days in IT, when the image of an army of clerks was used as an alternative to a computer system, to see what real benefits were being gained by using the system.

Outcome

Army of a thousand won't necessarily come up with an outright solution. It does, however, help you to examine different directions to move in. If an actual solution emerges, so much the better – otherwise, use it to feed into a technique from Chapter 5. The first stage may result in more questions that need answering – don't worry, this just means that you don't really understand your problem yet.

Variations

If this technique is used in a team, undertake each of the two stages individually first, then share the outcome, rather than doing the whole thing *en masse*. There aren't many significant variations here. The number 1,000 is arbitrary – there may be circumstances when dealing with huge numbers of real people that it should be magnified. The idea is that there are at least 10 or 20 times as much resource as you would have in reality.

Expertise:	✓✓
Direction setting:	✓✓✓
Idea generation:	✓✓
Problem solving:	✓✓
Fun:	✓✓

4.17 Solve a different problem

Preparation:	Find a selection of verbal puzzles.
Running time:	5 to 10 minutes.
Resources:	None.
Teams:	Individual / team.

This technique broadens thinking and so makes it easier to develop a broader set of questions. It has an advantage that the process itself can be used as a form of stimulation for idea generation.

To start this process, share with the group (or yourself if you are doing this alone) a verbal puzzle. There are many puzzle books available that have these in and they provide excellent source material. If you want to keep a business focus then you could take lateral thinking puzzles from Edward de Bono's book *Lateral Thinking* or Paul Sloane's *The Leader's Guide to Lateral Thinking* (Kogan Page). The only real requirements are that the set up of the puzzle is short and that the solution is not immediately obvious. Discuss methodologies for solving the problem with the group. Make a note of these. Generate genuine solutions. Make a note of these.

You could stop here and just describe the exercise as a warm up. It would be more useful to move on a step and to take the methodologies and the solutions that you have listed as stimulation for the generation of more 'how to' questions.

Feedback

This exercise appeals to some people and is a significant turn off for others. It is not one to push hard if you have a group (or you are an individual) that does not react well to puzzles. Give it a short session and if it's working well and being productive, then allow it to run for longer.

Outcome

Exercises like this can feel like a waste of time (which is one good reason for using the output as stimulation), but they are really useful for tuning the thinking process and getting people to think of more than the immediate and obvious solutions that present themselves.

Variations

There are a number of variations already mentioned in terms of where you go with the output and how long you spend on this. Another variation would be to use physical puzzles rather than verbal ones. These tend to be more engaging, but require a significantly higher level of preparation.

Expertise: ✓✓
Direction setting: ✓✓✓
Idea generation: ✓✓
Problem solving: ✓✓✓
Fun: ✓✓✓

4.18 Restatement

Preparation:	Initial 'how to' statement.
Running time:	Five minutes.
Resources:	Flip charts.
Teams:	Team.

This technique uses a specific approach to get the participants to recast the 'how to' statement that is used to initialize the process. As such, it only works as a second phase of question development rather than in generating an initial question.

Begin by asking the members of the group to produce at least one restatement each of the problem that uses none of the nouns, verbs or adjectives in the original and that, ideally, has a radically different slant on the problem. These restatements can be collected by asking for them and listing them on the flip chart, or by giving flip chart paper to the group and asking them to write up their own with four or five people sharing a sheet. The first works best with small groups and has the advantage of everyone hearing everyone else's restatement. The second is more efficient when the group is large, but it does require you to allow time for perusal of the results.

Feedback

This is a very simple technique and may seem like a statement of the obvious when you start. It is worth emphasizing the requirement for a radically different slant and stressing the strength that this will add to the final outcome.

Outcome

Despite being very basic, this works remarkably well as a way of broadening the range of questions being attacked. You will find a high degree of overlap in the 'how to' statements generated and you may want to remove duplications. If you do, make sure the group buy into this as they may see subtle differences between statements that look identical to you.

Variations

You can obviously vary how long you spend and how you collect the output, but the basic technique doesn't lend itself to significant change.

Expertise: ✓
Direction setting: ✓✓✓
Idea generation: ✓
Problem solving: ✓✓
Fun: ✓✓

4.19 Mud slinging

Preparation: None.
Running time: 5 to 10 minutes.
Resources: None.
Teams: Individual/team.

This technique is useful for product development, but does not generate much that can be used in other areas.

All that is needed is to agree on the company's most successful product or service, and to throw mud at it. In other words, to generate areas in which this star product is actually useless.

Having slung mud at this product, you then have available to you a whole list of areas of development that would make the product better. All you need to do is to rephrase them as 'how to' statements.

You may find that with many of the criticisms generated, you are not actually talking about enhancements to the existing product that was your starting point, but that an entirely new product would be needed to address the requirement. This is a good thing in that it broadens your areas of questioning.

Feedback

This is a fun and high-energy exercise. It is extremely good at generating new areas of investigation when developing a product. It is pretty useless at tackling other sorts of problems.

Outcome

The problem you are most likely to face in using this technique is volume. You will generate a huge number of alternative questions and approaches, and you will need to line up a selection process of some sort to whittle these down. See the end of the next chapter, from item 5.50, for some useful techniques.

Variations

Remember that product and service can be very broad terms. If you don't produce anything physical, or if you are an internal service department within an organization, then you will be able to adapt the definitions to suit you. If you really can't think of anything you produce or any service you provide, then you should be thinking of whether you really have a role to fulfil or not.

Expertise:	✓
Direction setting:	✓✓✓
Idea generation:	✓✓✓
Problem solving:	✓
Fun:	✓✓✓

4.20 Questions race

Preparation: None.
Running time: Five minutes.
Resources: Two (or more) flip charts.
Teams: Team.

This is a technique that only works for groups and taps into the natural competitiveness that appears whenever teams are formed. The group should be split into two or more teams with a flipchart available for each team.

Line the teams up some distance away from the flip charts and give each team a flip chart pen. Their task is to write as many questions (in the form of 'how to' statements) as they can in a given time. Stress that the pen is the baton in a relay race and that they must stay behind a line until they have hold of the baton.

Feedback

Much of the success of this technique is in the set-up. If you engender a spirit of competition before the race starts, then the participants will push themselves harder to think of questions. Some form of small prize or incentive would be appropriate.

Outcome

This technique often generates a lot of questions that are of no great use for the idea development phase. There will be a few questions generated, however, that will significantly change the focus of the problem.

Variations

Some other rules you may want to impose are that all 'how to' statements should be legible and should make sense. To speed things up, you can drop the words 'how to' or can write them in shorthand as H2. You may also want to disallow any duplicate questions on a team's board. You will obviously stress that the referee's decision is final and no arguments will be acceptable (you could even have a stock of red and yellow cards ready just in case). Although we have included this race as a question generator, we have also used it in the past as an idea generator. Indeed, adapting the basic notion of a relay race to flip charts is limited only by your imagination.

Expertise:	✓✓
Direction setting:	✓✓✓
Idea generation:	✓✓
Problem solving:	✓✓
Fun:	✓✓✓

4.21 Whiteboard

Preparation:	None.
Running time:	Five minutes.
Resources:	A whiteboard with enough pens for everyone in the group to have one.
Teams:	Team (no more than 20 people).

This technique tries to attack the generation of questions as a problem in its own right. It uses the words that people associate with the problem as stimulation for generating questions.

The process is to have everyone write all of the words they associate with the problem on to the whiteboard. The issue is that they will all be doing this at the same time. It sounds like an unnecessary complication to have everyone writing at the same time, but this will both increase the energy level of the group and promote a feeling of competition.

When everyone has written on the board you will find that you have a total mess of words. These can be used as stimulation for the generation of 'how to' questions. Probably the best way to do this is to take a couple of words and generate 'how to' questions from them to make sure that everybody understands what is required. Then have everyone work individually, each generating at least three questions.

Feedback

This is a good technique to use if energy levels are sagging. It is very effective at generating questions and also injects energy into the group. You may find that some people hang back from the battle around the whiteboard and wait their turn. Be prepared to encourage them in to take their part.

Outcome

As with some of the earlier techniques, the selection of 'how to' questions becomes an issue with this technique and you need to have thought this through before you use it.

Variations

This technique has proved as effective for idea generation as well as question generation. With a very large group you might be able to use multiple whiteboards, but this is likely to require multiple facilitators if the process is to be managed adequately. It will also significantly lengthen the running time, as information from the different sessions is combined.

Expertise:	✓✓
Direction setting:	✓✓✓
Idea generation:	✓✓
Problem solving:	✓✓
Fun:	✓✓

Techniques 2

What's the answer?

The techniques in this (largest) section are heavy-duty problem solvers and idea generators. When using these techniques, the participant(s) will already have a reasonable idea of what they are trying to achieve, but not of how to achieve it.

5.1 Challenging assumptions

Preparation:	None.
Running time:	15 minutes.
Resources:	None.
Teams:	Individual/team.

Creativity is all about breaking unwarranted assumptions. This technique, one of the oldest in the creativity armoury, does so directly. Consider your problem or requirement. What is the prime assumption in it? What is absolutely essential, absolutely key to the requirement? Now, consider what would happen if this assumption wasn't true. For example, if you were trying to improve the profitability of an accountancy firm, how would you do it if the company didn't employ any accountants? If you were trying to come up with a new wall covering, what would you do if you weren't allowed to use any colours? Or attach it to walls?

Once you have assessed the implications of your switch of assumption, feed the results back into your problem. Okay, you can actually have colours in your wall coverings, but what did you discover by looking at the possibilities without colouring? How could you apply these possibilities (with or without colours)? How could you modify them to fit your market? How could you combine them with existing approaches to come up with something different?

Feedback

Like many techniques, the hardest part here is the leap back from the implications of the broken assumption to the real problem. This gets much easier with practice – in fact, we recommend that you practise these techniques whether or not you have a specific problem, just to make the associations easier. See page 8 in Chapter 2 for more detail on making associations.

Outcome

It isn't always possible to identify a key assumption, but it is amazing how often that the result of relaxing one is to open up totally the problem, making solutions plentiful – and with an easy link back to the real world.

Variations

Only work on one assumption at a time, but try another if you hit a brick wall. Most problems will actually have several key assumptions. Make the assumptions specific rather than woolly.

Expertise:	✓✓
Direction setting:	✓✓
Idea generation:	✓✓✓✓
Problem solving:	✓✓✓✓
Fun:	✓✓

5.2 Distortion

Preparation:	None.
Running time:	15 minutes.
Resources:	None.
Teams:	Individual/team.

Most problems have clear dimensions. They might be spatial, numerical or time oriented. For example, if we wanted to improve a supermarket's checkouts, dimensions might include number of counters, number of staff, number of customers, size of checkout and times the checkout was open.

In this exercise, you will take a key dimension of your problem and distort it. Make it much bigger, or much smaller, than it currently is. In the checkout example, you might look at the implications of having 1 checkout or 1,000. Having one customer or a million. Having checkouts the size of a matchbox or the size of a warehouse. Opening a checkout for one second or one year at a time. Don't try to cover everything – choose one dimension and stick with it.

When you have noted down the implications of the distortion, look back at the real world. For example, if you had chosen a matchbox checkout, you could use a direct output from the distortion – smaller checkouts just for baskets, making more space. Or you can look at an implication like having tiny staff. In the real world, tiny staff would mean lots of room behind the checkout. Is the space given to the employee getting in the way of giving good service? Could a change in space improve things? And so on.

Feedback

With some problems, usually the very people-oriented, it is difficult to find an appropriate dimension. If so, try another technique. It is also possible that the dimension chosen doesn't work very well. Choose another, but make sure you have really examined the possibilities first – don't skip around just because the distortion seems uncomfortable; it is supposed to.

Outcome

When this technique works well, it works very well, because the dimension selected was a major restraint in your thinking.

Variations

Resist the inclination to handle multiple distortions in a single group, but with multiple teams it is well worth parcelling out the distortions to get a wider range of suggestions.

Expertise:	✓✓
Direction setting:	✓✓
Idea generation:	✓✓✓✓
Problem solving:	✓✓✓
Fun:	✓✓

5.3 Reversal

Preparation:	None.
Running time:	15 minutes.
Resources:	None.
Teams:	Individual/team.

Reversal is the extreme case of *Distortion* (5.2). Here, instead of taking an aspect of the problem and distorting it, we turn the problem inside out to reverse actually what we are trying to do. For example, if the requirement were to improve the company's position in a published league table, reversal would be to think 'what could we do to make our position in the league table worse'.

Spend five minutes brainstorming ideas to actively negate your 'how to' statement. Then look at the implications of the ideas you have generated. Worryingly often, these will be practices that are actually undertaken in your company. A classic example is the problem 'how to improve communications within our company'. Many of the suggestions for 'how to make communications fail in our company' seem already to be underway in many large companies. One outcome, therefore, is to modify or stop these existing practices. Other deductions will be more indirect, looking at the implications of the negative suggestions. For example, fitting a muzzle (to stop communications) may make you think of someone holding a mobile phone to their face.

Feedback

Make sure that you are prepared to go beyond the obvious, both in the negative suggestions and how these are applied back to the real problem. It's easy to simply list the obvious positive ideas in reverse, then turn them around again. But you are looking for something more than the obvious when using creativity techniques.

Outcome

This is not a good technique for new product development, but it is great for overcoming obstacles and other aspects of dealing with general problems.

Variations

With a group you can split the team into 'bad guys', looking to make the proposition fail, and 'good guys' looking to reverse the bad guys' ideas and convert them into something useful. This can be made into a challenge – try to find something so negative that the 'good guys' can't use it.

Expertise:	✓✓
Direction setting:	✓✓
Idea generation:	✓
Problem solving:	✓✓✓✓
Fun:	✓✓✓

5.4 Fantasy

Preparation:	None.
Running time:	10 minutes.
Resources:	None.
Teams:	Individual/team.

The *Fantasy* technique is the practical application of the daydream. Sit back and say, 'wouldn't it be wonderful if...'. Imagine that there were no obstacles, no limits to your abilities. What would you do? What would the solution look like? One of the real problems with coming up with a creative solution to a problem is the left brain/right brain split. Whether or not this alleged phenomenon is true, we do seem to separate logical, sequential activity and 'artistic', holistic activity. Creativity often requires a step into the fuzzier right brain – if you can move out of problem solving mode, usually a left-brain activity, and into daydreaming, you have a much better chance of reaching a creative solution.

As usual, when you have some results you may need to modify them to make them more practical, or just use them as a stepping-off point which makes you think of a different, but associated, practical solution which still remains creative.

Feedback

It is absolutely essential to get out of left brain, problem solving mode before this technique will work. You may find it helpful to have a two minute distraction from the problem – glance at the newspaper, go outside, do anything to get off track.

Outcome

This technique will often not generate a refined solution. Instead, it is good at providing a broad sweep of solution space, which can then be modified to a final result. Many will find it difficult to lose logicality in a business context. For them, one of the other techniques that more explicitly forces you out of your conventional pattern will be more appropriate.

Variations

As an alternative approach, try drawing a picture of a solution to your problem. If you've got problems with drawing, or want to make this more a group activity, collect a set of appealing images (catalogues and Sunday supplements are usually a good source), cut them out and make a collage of a solution. See *Draw it* (5.28) for an alternative approach to this variant.

Expertise:	✓✓✓
Direction setting:	✓✓
Idea generation:	✓✓✓
Problem solving:	✓✓✓
Fun:	✓✓

5.5 Someone else's view

Preparation:	None.
Running time:	15 minutes.
Resources:	None.
Teams:	Individual/team.

As a big blockage to creativity is tunnel vision, this technique uses another person's opinion to provide a different solution. Pick another person – historical, fictional, topical or just a role (like 'plumber' or 'brain surgeon'). It doesn't matter who, as long as they're a long way from you in experience and outlook. To make it easier, we've provided a list in Appendix 2 (page 185), but feel free to pick someone yourself. You needn't know a lot about this person – just enough to have a caricature of who they are or were.

Now imagine that you are this person. Get under their skin. Spend a few moments getting the feel of being them. Then address your problem. How would your adopted persona deal with the problem? How would they understand (or misunderstand) what it was all about? Get together a good list of ideas from this person's point of view.

Finally, pull the suggestions back to the real world. Are they practical? Could they be modified? What do they make you think of?

Feedback

It is common for participants to reject a persona because they don't feel comfortable with it, or they feel it's unsuitable, or they have no idea who the person is. Only the last argument is valid. As long as the participant has a vague idea who they are meant to be, the persona will be valuable – and the less 'suitable' for the problem the better.

Outcome

Provided the participants throw themselves into this technique, it is reliable. Without inhibitions, it is very effective.

Variations

In a team, each member could take the same person, but it is better if each takes a different one. Team members should think of their ideas separately, then pool them. At a large event with more time, this technique can be enhanced by giving participants the opportunity to dress up, maintaining their persona for a considerable period of time. As a variant, imagine phoning up an old friend with whom you've lost touch and asking for their views.

Expertise: ✓✓
Direction setting: ✓✓
Idea generation: ✓✓✓
Problem solving: ✓✓✓✓
Fun: ✓✓✓

5.6 Metaphor

Preparation:	None.
Running time:	10 to 15 minutes.
Resources:	None.
Teams:	Individual / team.

At the heart of all of creativity techniques is the notion that you need to be taken away from your problem to generate creative solutions. Otherwise, you could do so from a standing start without the aid of techniques. *Metaphor* is powerful because it can be the basis of a whole range of ways for tackling your issues, and because we all use metaphors in our understanding of the world.

At its simplest, all you need to do is to generate a metaphor or an analogy for your problem and then work on it. Say the problem is 'how to overtake our main competitor in sales', an obvious metaphor might be 'our problem is like a Grand Prix race'. You could then look at why this is the case, deriving associations from the metaphor. Equally, you could use a more obscure metaphor – 'our problem is like a bowl of porridge'. Now the initial task is constructing a set of justifications as to why the metaphor is valid. These can (and should) be as wild and tenuous as you like. Then use these justifications and the metaphor itself to generate associations.

Feedback

It is often tough to find a metaphor that really represents a problem. This shouldn't be an issue. If an obvious metaphor occurs to you, and it is sufficiently different from your problem that it will take you away from it, use it. If one does not occur, use any metaphor and force-fit a relationship. We have often used a list of topics (the random word list in Appendix 2, for example) and selected one at random.

Outcome

Metaphor is at the heart of the creative process. We have frequently run entire sessions based around a single metaphor. These sessions can then use additional techniques within the overall session, but the theme remains intact.

Variations

If working with a group, you can split into teams and challenge teams to find metaphors that other teams will be unable to use to generate ideas and then get them to do just that. This is one way of ensuring genuinely creative solutions.

Expertise: ✓✓✓
Direction setting: ✓✓
Idea generation: ✓✓✓✓
Problem solving: ✓✓✓✓
Fun: ✓✓

5.7 Random word

Preparation:	None.
Running time:	10 to 15 minutes.
Resources:	None.
Teams:	Individual/team.

This technique is many people's favourite. It often becomes the only creativity technique used because it is straightforward and effective. There is a real danger in developing a reliance on a single technique. Our whole thrust is to get you to move out of your regular tunnel of thinking. The last thing we want to do is to create a new tunnel. The selectors in Appendix 1 will help to ensure that you use a wide range of techniques.

Random word involves choosing a word at random, making as many associations with that word as you are able to and then relating these back to your problem. The word that you choose will usually be a noun, but need not be. It will usually be emotive, but need not be. It will certainly bring to mind a range of images and associations. To choose the word, you can use a book or a dictionary and allow them to fall open at random. We prefer using a pre-selected list of suitable words and choosing at random from that. To get you started, there is a list in Appendix 2 (page 184).

Feedback

Random word becomes a favourite for a reason. It works, and works well. It is easy to explain to others, and we would almost always use it as an early demonstrator of a creativity technique. Some people want to choose a word that is relevant to their problem. Don't do this. Use a random word – it will turn out to be appropriate.

Outcome

You will find that alone, or in groups, you have no trouble engaging with this technique. It will produce results.

Variations

If working with a group, you can make a show of the randomness by getting someone else to choose the word or call out a number to select from the list in Appendix 2. An alternative source of a random word is to input word-like nonsense into a computer spellchecker, then see what emerges. For a similar technique with quite different results, see *Two words* (5.45).

Expertise:	✓✓
Direction setting:	✓✓
Idea generation:	✓✓✓✓
Problem solving:	✓✓✓✓
Fun:	✓✓

5.8 Random picture

Preparation:	None.
Running time:	10 to 15 minutes.
Resources:	A selection of pictures from which to select, or one chosen at random.
Teams:	Individual/team.

Random picture involves selecting an image, then making any and every association that you can with that image and, finally, relating those associations back to your problem in the way that we examined in Chapter 2. How could the associations help with the problem? What types of solution do they make you think of? How could you change things to be like (or unlike) the associations?

Selecting suitable images requires a little thought. You should look for images that are not just a representation of a word. A photograph of a typewriter, for instance, will not give much more stimulation than the word typewriter. A picture of a typewriter with a bored secretary behind it, staring into space, would start off all sorts of stories in our minds.

One useful source of pictures is to buy a photography manual from a remaindered bookshop. You will find that you can pick up a book with thousands of images for a very low price. An alternative is to buy packs of art postcards. Generally, though, just put a random word into the image search of Google and pick the first rich image.

Feedback

This technique often proves slightly harder to get going than *Random word* (5.7), but generates a much richer set of associations. It can also be more enjoyable once it is going, because images seem to have more fun about them than a word.

Outcome

The associations generated by this technique will tend to include some very off-the-wall ones. These should be forced into the idea development phase as the ideas that result will be more original.

Variations

If working with a group, try splitting into teams and having a different image for each team. Postcards or mounted posters help here. Alternatives to this are random selection from an encyclopaedia (preferably electronic), which gives a very rich source of stimulation, or from a catalogue (particularly good for devising new products).

Expertise:	✓✓
Direction setting:	✓✓
Idea generation:	✓✓✓✓
Problem solving:	✓✓✓
Fun:	✓✓✓

5.9 Found objects

Preparation:	None.
Running time:	20 to 30 minutes.
Resources:	None.
Teams:	Team.

If you are spending anything more than an hour generating ideas, you will find that you hit a lull in focus and energy. You will need frequent breaks to avoid this, but another approach is to use a creativity technique that energizes. *Found objects* is an excellent technique for injecting energy and fun into a session and has the advantage that it is great at generating ideas, too.

To use it, simply get the group to leave the room and come back with something that they have individually found somewhere else. It could be something as mundane as a cigarette end. We have run sessions where participants have unplugged telephones, stolen a cleaner's trolley, taken pictures off walls or arrived with a whole tree in a pot.

They then need to be able to talk to the rest of their team about the object with emotion and passion. Why is this object important and why does it hold the answer to the problem? This level of passion can be quite funny when the object is a discarded sweet wrapper or a sheet of toilet paper.

As each individual speaks, the rest of the group should be making links back to the problem out of what they hear. They then share these links and build on them to produce solutions.

Feedback

This technique is most successful when you include in your set up an implied challenge to find a bizarre or surprising object. It generates a lot of laughter and the energy from this pushes through to the idea session.

Outcome

The two key outcomes of this technique are a change in the energy level and a collection of original ideas.

Variations

The technique works best as a small team exercise, but can be used with larger groups split into teams or even by yourself. In practice, though, the whole business feels very artificial when working alone. If you have to do so, you still should express your passion and emotion as most of the associations result from this stage, not from the object itself.

Expertise: ✓✓
Direction setting: ✓✓
Idea generation: ✓✓✓✓
Problem solving: ✓✓✓✓
Fun: ✓✓✓✓

5.10 Nonsense sentence

Preparation:	None.
Running time:	10 to 15 minutes.
Resources:	A list of nonsense sentences.
Teams:	Individual/team.

Nonsense sentence makes use of the brain's ability to create order out of chaos, even when no order really exists. It takes the idea behind *Random word* (5.7) one stage further, making use of a random sentence that has little or no meaning.

In Appendix 2 (page 185) you will find a list of nonsense sentences. By their very nature these are meaningless. Take a look at this list before reading through the rest of this technique, so that you understand the nature of what we are discussing. Select a nonsense sentence at random. Force meaning into it by discussing what this nonsense might mean. Get very specific in this discussion. Then make any and all associations that you can from this and finally relate these back to your problem in the way we describe in Chapter 2 (page 8).

Feedback

This is one of those techniques that can prove a great hit with a group or a real flop. Be prepared to drop it quickly if the group that you are working with does not relate to it. In introducing the technique, it might prove useful to give an example and to discuss what this might be before moving on to the real thing. This gives you the opportunity to inject meaning and to demonstrate how the brain can find order in chaos or meaning in something meaningless.

Outcome

If this works for you or your group it will prove extremely effective at generating ideas.

Variations

A useful product development technique is to make up semi-nonsense sentences. Include a product range, or potential product range, with a random situation and then use this as a stimulus. For instance, if you are involved in developing hair care products you might have, 'A hair care product for use on the beach' or, 'The army shampoo' or, 'Kitchen hair care'. These may mean nothing, but their development will result in new ideas.

Expertise:	✓✓
Direction setting:	✓✓
Idea generation:	✓✓✓
Problem solving:	✓✓✓
Fun:	✓✓

5.11 On this day

Preparation:	None.
Running time:	10 minutes.
Resources:	Dictionary of dates; paper and pens.
Teams:	Individual / team.

Look up today's date in a dictionary of dates. Pick out two or three entries that appeal because they are bizarre, exciting or just make you think of something. Typically, the dates in such lists represent an event in history, or the birth or death of a person. Imagine yourself present at the event, or being that person. How would you look at the problem? What would you do about it? What different perspectives would you get from being at the event, or from the sort of activity that was typical of this person? Would the period of history involved generate any misunderstandings?

Combine different ideas from different sources. Be prepared to treat them as a starting point, rather than a final solution.

Feedback

This technique is related to *Someone else's view* (5.5), but a number of factors make it feel quite different. The 'on this day' facts are interesting in their own right. There will often be parallels and reverses between the items in the list and the current day. And most of all, the mix of people and events gives a much richer source of inspiration. Just as a random picture gives much more than a random word, an event with all its associations will normally produce more than a single person.

Outcome

This technique often gives a wider range of ideas than similar techniques – and manages to be fun without the threatening aspects of role play that sometimes occur elsewhere.

Variations

If you don't have a dictionary of dates, or want a different type of stimulus, many CD-ROM based encyclopaedias have them, as do various online sites. The default approach is simply to try each of the events/people you picked. However, you could try combining them to interesting effect. What would the painter Gaugin do if he saw the first Zeppelin destroyed? What would Richard the Lionheart (or Harry Houdini) make of the first Olympic Games?

Expertise:	✓✓
Direction setting:	✓✓✓
Idea generation:	✓✓
Problem solving:	✓✓✓✓
Fun:	✓✓✓

5.12 Cool site

Preparation:	None.
Running time:	10 minutes.
Resources:	Access to the internet (ideally visible to all participants).
Teams:	Individual/team.

Many internet pages list a 'cool site' – a regularly changing recommendation of something interesting, challenging or just weird. The ever-changing nature of these sites means that they are a useful source of random stimulation. They also provide a whole mix of words, images and even sounds to generate association and stimulation.

As with any reference to the internet some of these addresses will be out of date by the time you read this book. You will find up-to-date listings at **http://www.cul.co.uk/creative**. Another useful site at the time of printing was: **http://www. coolsiteoftheday.com**.

Or look on Google (**http://www.google.co.uk**) or Yahoo (**http://www.yahoo.com**) for: computer and internet; world wide web; searching the web; indices to web documents; random links and sites of the day and sites of the week. This provides long lists of current sites that provide a random jump or a cool site service. Many of these are very specific, eg, medical, gay, family, adult oriented. Once you have a site, use it like *Random picture* (5.8) to generate associations, then link them back to the problem.

Feedback

To use this process with a group, it is advisable to download the site before displaying it. This has three advantages: first, you know it is suitable; second, you know it will work; and third, you know it will be faster.

Outcome

The nature of the web means that you are likely to hit on some extremely effective stimulation. Careful editing in advance can enhance this further. As with all forms of random stimulation, don't be tempted to find a site that is relevant to the problem; this will decrease the effectiveness of the exercise. The aim of editing is to provide more stimulation, not relevance to the problem.

Variations

If working with a group, you can either display a site for everyone to work on or you can use individual computers for people to find their own stimulation.

Expertise:	✓✓
Direction setting:	✓✓
Idea generation:	✓✓✓✓
Problem solving:	✓✓✓✓
Fun:	✓✓✓

5.13 Headlines

Preparation:	Newspaper collection.
Running time:	10 minutes.
Resources:	A collection of current (today's) newspapers.
Teams:	Individual/team.

Many of the stimuli that are used in techniques in this book provide an immediate image that makes a whole set of associations happen in your head. This is, in some ways, the job of the headline writer in newspapers. For this reason, headlines make an effective form of stimulation.

Take a selection of newspapers, ideally today's for immediacy, but use a previous day's if this will help you to feel better prepared. Cut from these newspapers the headlines without the text of the story and distribute them to the participants.

Have the participants spend a few minutes working on their own to generate a set of associations that occur to them as a result of the headline. Stress to them that even if they know what the story is about this is not of interest. It is the words in the headline that are the source of inspiration for them.

List all of the associations from the whole group. Now relate these back to your problem area and so use them as a source of ideas.

Feedback

This is another form of pseudo-random stimulation that takes an area removed from your problem back to your problem area. It is effective because of the wide range of associations that most headlines will generate.

Outcome

Some individuals will have trouble with this technique, either because of their headline or because of the way their minds work. Be prepared to allow people to team up to share headlines and ideas. For most people this will be a great source of new ideas.

Variations

You can distribute individual headlines or display a single headline on an overhead transparency. Instead of just taking the headlines as they are, you could cut and paste dissimilar headlines together to form your own bizarre versions. Web users will find news headlines available from a multitude of sources online. Try **http://www.bbc.co.uk**, for example.

Expertise: ✓✓
Direction setting: ✓✓
Idea generation: ✓✓✓
Problem solving: ✓✓✓
Fun: ✓✓

5.14 Quotations

Preparation:	None.
Running time:	10 minutes.
Resources:	Dictionary of quotations; paper and pens.
Teams:	Individual/team.

Look for key words in the problem statement. Use a dictionary of quotations to come up with some choice quotes that involve these key words. There should be at least three but not more than seven. If you can't find the exact key words, consider variants of them. Write the quotations down, ideally on flip chart paper. Put them somewhere anyone involved in the exe rcise can see them. Now look at the quotations. Consider them as advice on solving your problem. Look for suggestions of an idea in what they refer to. Is there something about their words or context that makes you think of a solution?

Feedback

While belonging to the family of techniques which use a random stimulation, this approach is interesting because it uses key words related to the problem, but the quotations, out of context, will push those original key words in totally different directions. The use of quotations helps creative thinking because there is often humour, ambiguity or simple interest in the remark, all of which will help the creative process.

Outcome

Quotations is a good technique to use with participants who are uncomfortable with creativity techniques, because there is a sense of consulting the wisdom of others, however spurious this may be. The results, however, are certainly not restricted to mundane ideas, as many of the quotations will be derived from a totally different world to that in which the problem exists.

Variations

Instead of selecting by subject, select by person – think of someone whose opinion you'd like to consult. If the topic is known in advance, the quotations can be pre-written on flip charts to avoid wasting time looking them up. Note that many people are not familiar with dictionaries of quotations and may need some guidance. Online dictionaries of quotations are even better, as a full word search can be used. Rather than selecting the most provocative quotes, an alternative is to choose one at random (second in the list, say), use that one, then choose another.

Expertise:	✓
Direction setting:	✓✓✓
Idea generation:	✓✓✓✓
Problem solving:	✓✓✓✓
Fun:	✓✓✓

5.15 Squirrel box

Preparation:	Produce a squirrel box.
Running time:	10 minutes.
Resources:	Squirrel box.
Teams:	Individual/team.

This technique requires considerable preparation, but once prepared can be used without warning. Get hold of a shoebox, or similar container (a fancy plastic or wooden box will look more professional, but won't work any better). Put into it anything that raises the eyebrows. It can be a small object, a newspaper cutting, a photograph, part of a cereal box, as long as it is unusual and interesting or entertaining. Make maintenance of your box a background task. Whenever you see anything appropriate, squirrel it away.

When it comes to the creativity session, pick two items out at random. Look at them and/or read them through. What do they make you think of separately and together? How would some interaction between the two solve your problem or come up with a new idea?

Feedback

The tactile nature of fishing the objects out of a box is all part of the experience – don't resort to sticking the items into a scrapbook. If possible, cycle old stuff out as you use it. The flow of new content will stop the technique from growing stale.

Outcome

This is a particularly enjoyable association technique, which will appeal to those who like squirreling away fascinating facts, silly stories and bizarre photographs.

Variations

You can use the sort of book of bizarre happenings that you will sometimes find in a remaindered bookshop as a starter pack for your squirrel box, but cut out items from it, don't use the book directly. If using this technique with a group, a good warm-up is to refer to the box as a brain box. Have a second identical box with a cauliflower coated in gel in it. Ask someone to feel inside without looking. When they react say, 'whoops, wrong brain box' and substitute the real thing.

Expertise: ✓✓
Direction setting: ✓✓
Idea generation: ✓✓✓
Problem solving: ✓✓✓✓
Fun: ✓✓✓

5.16 Set it to music

Preparation:	Get together a stack of mixed CDs.
Running time:	10 minutes.
Resources:	A CD player and a stack of mixed CDs.
Teams:	Individual/team.

Start with a very eclectic set of CDs – make sure there's a good mix of classical and popular music. Choose a CD at random, then a random track. Many CD players have a random function that will help with this. Spend a minute taking an overview of your problem statement and any information you have about the problem area. Then play two or three minutes of the track. As you listen to the music, have the problem area in the back of your mind. Is there anything in the words (if any) that sparks off an idea? Does the music itself make you think of anything, or remind you of anything that has happened? Make use of these associations to establish new possibilities.

Feedback

There is an element here of using a random stimulus to generate associations, where you might find it useful to check the guidance on associations in Chapter 2 (page 8). However, using music is different to a random word or picture, as the act of listening to music – really listening, not just having music in the background – can itself provide a vehicle for moving away from your previous frame of mind.

Outcome

This technique produces less volume than the other random stimulation techniques, but the combination of the music as stimulus and as distraction means that you will often achieve something more radical than with the alternatives.

Variations

It is not necessary to use a piece of music you are unfamiliar with – listening to a familiar piece can generate powerful associations – but it is important not to use the same piece of music repeatedly as it becomes a rut in its own right. An interesting variant with a team is that each team member should choose a CD for another team member, consciously trying to make it as far away from their known tastes as possible. Tapes can be used, but CDs are preferable as it makes randomly selecting tracks much easier.

Expertise:	✓
Direction setting:	✓✓
Idea generation:	✓✓✓✓
Problem solving:	✓✓✓
Fun:	✓✓

5.17 Da Vinci scribbles

Preparation:	None.
Running time:	10 minutes.
Resources:	Pencil and paper or flip chart and pens.
Teams:	Individual / team.

This makes use of a technique invented by Leonardo da Vinci – just to show that the business of creativity techniques is not exactly new. Sit down at a pad with a soft pencil in your hand. Close your eyes and start to scribble. Not the scratchy scribble of a child – imagine that you are an artist, sketching in an outline of something. Only don't direct the pencil, just let it flow across the page. When you feel you've scribbled enough, open your eyes. Look at the image you have generated.

What does it make you think of? What does it remind you of? How might you use it in your problem? What characteristics of it are appropriate to a solution? What sort of new product does it imply (or could you use to deal with it)? Be imaginative – let your mind wander over just what this scribble might be.

Feedback

Leonardo used this method to come up with new inventions which, considering his track record, makes it quite a promising technique. If you have problems seeing anything in your picture, think of modern art – what title might you give your artwork in a gallery? Look for suggestions in the shapes and sub-patterns.

Outcome

This technique is marginally better for coming up with new ideas than solving problems, but it is quite often a source of a solution.

Variations

In a group, you could each generate your own picture, or have a single person draw on a flip chart, then all of the group can individually think about what it implies before sharing their thoughts. Other old techniques this is reminiscent of are seeing pictures in cloud formations or in an open fire. Given appropriate surroundings, either of these will make an effective variant.

Expertise: ✓✓
Direction setting: ✓✓
Idea generation: ✓✓✓✓
Problem solving: ✓✓✓
Fun: ✓✓

5.18 Inside view

Preparation:	None.
Running time:	10 minutes.
Resources:	None.
Teams:	Individual / team.

In this technique you will be getting into the heart of the problem – in fact, imagining you are part of the problem itself. For example, if you wanted to come up with a new hand-held electronic device, think, 'What would it feel like to be one of these products? What would I like? What would irritate me?' Build a psychological profile of your target. Similarly, if you are trying to solve a problem, get into the 'mind' of the obstacle (if you know what it is). If not, pick something that typifies the problem itself and think your way into it.

Use the insights you gain from this insider's view to come up with new ways of developing a solution to your requirements.

Feedback

There can be some resistance to this technique initially, because it involves thinking like an inanimate (or, at least, non-human) object. At its extreme, you might even be required to think like something insubstantial – sunlight, or a bad odour. This isn't as hard as it sounds. In *Imagination Engineering* (see Chapter 6 for more details) we include an example of a story written from the point of view of a nasturtium. This is definitely one where practice helps.

Outcome

The inside view can be very illuminating, because we always see situations from our own viewpoint. By looking from the inside out, the problem will appear very different – and hence this can be an extremely powerful technique.

Variations

In a sense this is a variation on *Someone else's view* (5.5), but with very different outcomes because of the way it uses non-human resources and resources that are involved with the problem. With a group, you can usually split the internal viewpoint to give several approaches. For example, if you were looking to design a new air freshener, you could do it from the point of view of the freshener itself, the bad smell, the air molecules, any fabrics in the room, and so on.

Expertise: ✓✓
Direction setting: ✓✓
Idea generation: ✓✓✓✓
Problem solving: ✓✓✓✓
Fun: ✓✓✓

5.19 Shades

Preparation:	None.
Running time:	10 minutes.
Resources:	Adjective list.
Teams:	Individual/team.

This technique is the sort of thing that gives creativity a bad name – which is a shame, because it really works. You begin with a list of adjectives – feel free to come up with your own, or use our list from Appendix 2 (page 186). Pick one at random. Now consider the proposition, 'our problem is xxx', where xxx is the adjective. For example, if the adjective was pink, what would be the implications of the problem being pink? What is it about the problem that makes it pink? Your natural reaction might be NOTHING! There is nothing pink about, 'how to reduce the impact of foreign exchange rates on our company'. But then you might start to think about pink. Like the *Financial Times*, and the diluted (once red) ex-communist bloc countries, and even pink underwear in the Folies Bergère. Look at the associations this pink-shaded problem has generated. Now relate these back to the problem, and its solution.

Feedback

This technique doesn't require a lot of expertise, but it does require a significant amount of faith in believing that creativity techniques work – otherwise it's just plain silly. It is best used once an individual or group has used one of the more straightforward techniques.

Outcome

Despite any reluctance to use it, this is a very powerful technique that can generate a whole range of very different suggestions.

Variations

As an alternative, you might like to apply the adjective to the solution. Instead of saying the problem is pink (or whatever), say the (as yet unknown) solution is pink. What are the implications then? It is best not to use both variations in sequence, as there is inevitably a lot of overlap, but with a group it may well be worth splitting the group into two and have one apply the adjective to the problem, the other to the solution. In a team, this technique benefits from individuals generating their ideas first, then sharing them.

Expertise:
Direction setting:
Idea generation:
Problem solving:
Fun:

5.20 Problem perfect

Preparation:	None.
Running time:	Five minutes.
Resources:	None.
Teams:	Individual/team.

Most other techniques in this section are about generating solutions to a problem. This technique is about trying to find a way to make your problem state desirable. This does not mean saying, 'just cope' or, 'learn to live with it'. It involves asking what would have to change in the world to make your problem a desirable state of affairs.

Let's illustrate this with a generic example. Assume that your problem is falling profits in a small business. Most techniques will look at ways of increasing profits. Here you will look at why lower profit provides an advantage, then take this forward as a solution. Lower profits could be good if the profitability was higher. If costs and overheads can be reduced, having lower profits may not matter because the rate of return is high. This may not be true, but it gives a starting point. Lower profits will lead to lower taxation. This gives us an alternative direction: lowering tax overhead.

There are two possible outcomes from this technique: being happier to live with the problem; or finding an alternative way of tackling it.

Feedback

This technique is useful for apparently intractable problems. However, there is a danger that those helping to solve the problem will fall into the mindset that there is nothing to be done about the problem itself and, therefore, see no point in using other techniques to tackle it.

Outcome

You will not always generate ways of learning to live with your problem. You will almost certainly generate ways of tackling your problem from another angle. Despite this, the starting point is always the intent to find a solution that involves living with the problem.

Variations

With more time, *Problem perfect* can be used in two explicit stages: how could you change the world to live with it (set of solutions), then how could you change the world so it goes away (second set of solutions) The outcome of the two sessions can then be combined.

Expertise: ✓✓✓
Direction setting: ✓✓✓
Idea generation: ✓✓
Problem solving: ✓✓✓
Fun: ✓✓

5.21 Frontiers

Preparation:	None.
Running time:	Five minutes.
Resources:	None.
Teams:	Individual/team.

This technique is designed to bring out the frontier spirit, using (as a certain TV series put it) the final frontier as a setting. Imagine you are on a space mission on an unknown planet. Spend a minute thinking about this totally alien environment. Now what if your problem or idea requirement came up here, on this planet. What would you do? How would you solve it? Bear in mind your isolation from the rest of humanity and the sorts of science fiction technology you might be able to apply. You might need to modify slightly the problem to fit your environment, but try to fit quite closely.

Feedback

Make sure the participants get into the spirit of this exercise. It doesn't matter if they don't like science fiction, or know nothing about it, the idiom is too strongly imbedded in modern culture to be ineffective. If there is any difficulty fitting the problem into your alien planet, modify it. For example, if your problem requires customers, then have little green men, and so forth. Be prepared to use every cliché in the book.

Outcome

Frontiers works best with one or more people who are really prepared to let go and let their imagination run wild. For that reason, it tends to work best with those who have some experience of creativity techniques. The combination of the alien environment, lack of contact with Earth and the imagined technology can result in some spectacular ideas. They may, of course, then need bringing back to Earth, but make sure that making them practical doesn't also make them mundane.

Variations

Frontiers can be worked alone, but is best as a group exercise, sparking ideas off each other. With more time available, more effort can be put into developing a scenario before going ahead with the exercise. One effective way to do this is to give each participant a copy of a science fiction short story to read the previous day. This will then be used as the scenario.

Expertise:	✓✓✓
Direction setting:	✓✓✓
Idea generation:	✓✓
Problem solving:	✓✓✓✓
Fun:	✓✓✓

5.22 **Attributes**

Preparation:	Getting hold of catalogues.
Running time:	10 minutes.
Resources:	A selection of catalogues with a wide range of products in them.
Teams:	Individual/team.

This and a few other techniques that follow make use of the fact that your problem is actually made up of a series of sub-elements. Even if you are dealing with product development, rather than idea generation or problem solving, you still have a series of attributes attached to the product.

Take a selection of catalogues and find a way of randomly selecting products. Letting the catalogue fall open in your hands will suffice. Take a few products (three to six) and select a single attribute from each. Attributes could be the colour, the texture, the power, the functions or anything else about them that takes your fancy. Now combine those attributes into the solution to your problem. If you are dealing with new product development this is relatively easy to do. If you are solving a problem it seems harder, but isn't. You simply need to build those attributes into your solution in the way that we have used associations elsewhere (see Chapter 2, page 8 for more information). Think how your solution could have these attributes. Think what other things you know (not just the items in the catalogues) have these attributes. Make use of your experience.

Feedback

While ideally suited to product development, this technique works well for more general problem solving. It often proves fun, particularly if you are not altogether random in your product selection and engineer some odd combinations. Be prepared to reselect if the combination is too tame.

Outcome

You will find some new avenues of thought with this technique and have a laugh or two on the way.

Variations

Attributes works well with teams or individuals. If using with teams, one spin that you could put on it is to compete to see how many attributes can be built into one solution. With more time, an intermediate phase, especially effective with groups, can be to construct a picture of something (anything) which embodies all these attributes and use this to spark off your thinking.

Expertise:	✓✓✓
Direction setting:	✓✓✓
Idea generation:	✓✓✓
Problem solving:	✓✓✓
Fun:	✓✓

5.23 Kid's play

Preparation:	Appropriate surroundings
Running time:	10 minutes.
Resources:	One child, aged between 7 and 12.
Teams:	Individual/team.

A very powerful technique that does require some preparation. Children are great creativity resources. They do not have the preconceptions about what is possible (or silly) that adults do and, accordingly, will come up with a range of ideas and solutions that are beyond the scope of adults. Of course, their ideas will be impractical, but they make superb starting points.

Using children is not a trivial issue. Any involvement of children in a business process must take account of the appropriate laws. The best approach is to formulate the input, let someone take it home to a child, get a response, and use that response the next day. The child should be given some context, phrased in a way they will understand without being patronizing. Try to make the exercise a game for them – trying to think of ten different ways to do this, or five new things to sell in this sort of shop.

Feedback

This isn't an attempt to get hold of cheap child labour – children will only give creative input if they are enjoying themselves. The age limit is significant. Below six or seven, the child will not have enough experience of the world, or vocabulary to deal with the problem. Once into their teens, creativity is closing down fast, and they are less likely to want to take part.

Outcome

This technique can be quite hard to implement, not because it is practically difficult, but because we are reluctant to accept guidance from children. We are culturally programmed to expect the ideas of children to be silly, yet they will often be particularly fresh. They will need refining, but not discarding. Children's ideas will often spark something completely different by association, too. Don't be afraid to chain-on from the child's suggestion.

Variations

Consider working with a local primary school as a resource exchange. See if they'd be interested in hearing something about your work, or going on a factory tour, or having some old office equipment in exchange for an idea session.

Expertise: ✓
Direction setting: ✓✓
Idea generation: ✓✓✓✓
Problem solving: ✓✓✓✓
Fun: ✓✓✓

5.24 **Components**

Preparation:	None.
Running time:	10 to 15 minutes.
Resources:	None.
Teams:	Individual/team.

Every problem you face has components that contribute to it and make it more or less soluble. These components get ignored because they are part of a bigger issue.

This technique involves breaking the problem down into its component parts and then tackling those components one at a time.

Start with a clear description of your problem and then, individually or in a group, break that problem down into its component parts. For instance, your problem might be how to make better use of space in your small garden. Some obvious components to this are the features (those that are there – fixed and changeable, those that you want), the uses (things you do and things that you want to do in the garden), time and space.

You would then take these in turn and try to generate some solutions to your bigger problem by using them. For instance, looking at the fixed features, you could consider how fixed they really are (could they be removed?), how you could extend their uses (for instance, using a tree as a place to hang baskets from or to support a seat). Looking at the variable features, which do you want, which could you remove? You would obviously do more than this with each component and cover all of the components.

Feedback

Somehow it is easier to solve a lot of small problems than one big one; this technique breaks problems down into bite-sized chunks. Used as explained, it is unlikely to give you any startlingly original solutions, but it will give you solutions to problems which seemed otherwise out of reach.

Outcome

With this technique, more than most of the others, you will end up with a comprehensive list of actions. Many of these, by the nature of the technique, will be easily done.

Variations

If you want more original ideas, as well as the bite-sized approach that this technique offers, then you could try breaking the problem into components and use a different technique on each of the components.

Expertise: ✓
Direction setting: ✓✓
Idea generation: ✓✓
Problem solving: ✓✓✓✓
Fun: ✓✓

5.25 Substitute

Preparation:	None.
Running time:	10 to 15 minutes.
Resources:	None.
Teams:	Individual/team.

This technique is identical to *Components* (5.24) with one fundamental difference. As with that technique, you must break the problem down into component parts but, instead of solving these components, you insert something different as the component and then solve that in relation to the overall problem.

Taking the example of making better use of space in a small garden we highlighted in *Components*, one key component was 'features'. We could replace 'features' with 'electricity', for example. So the issue for this component becomes, how can we make better use of the small garden by increasing the electricity?

At first glance this doesn't make sense, but as you treat this as a genuine problem some solutions start to appear. You could, for instance, improve the lighting and so have use of the garden for longer. You could heat a greenhouse or cloches and so have a longer growing season. You could support hanging baskets from the overhead power cables above the garden (or, if killing yourself is an issue, then you could hang them from another form of cable support). You could have a water feature, using an electric pump.

Some of the solutions that you generate (like the overhead power cable one) are likely to be non-starters. Do not throw them out; see how you can adapt them to make them workable.

Feedback

This technique feels very similar to *Components* when you start to use it, but it quickly becomes clear that it offers more creative solutions.

Outcome

You are still likely to generate a comprehensive set of actions from this technique, but you are likely to find that they are more creative (although in some cases less workable) than with *Components*.

Variations

This works with individuals or with teams. There is no need, and no great advantage, to use further creativity techniques on the component problems.

Expertise: ✓
Direction setting: ✓✓
Idea generation: ✓✓✓✓
Problem solving: ✓✓✓✓
Fun: ✓✓

5.26 It's a steal

Preparation:	May require mobility.
Running time:	30 minutes.
Resources:	Competitor information, internet access.
Teams:	Individual/team.

In an attempt to maintain company morale, it is not uncommon to give the impression that there is nothing to learn from your competitors, that 'we' are simply the best at everything. This is a serious mistake. For the first five minutes of the exercise, list who your competitors are. Consider general competitors of your company and specific competitors around the problem area. Consider unconnected companies who could be competitors, but don't happen to do that sort of business right now.

With your competitor portfolio in mind, spend a while on research. Check out any information you have on the competitor and anything there may be about them on the internet. If your business makes it practical to visit a competitor's premises, and you have the time, do so. Always be looking with your specific problem in mind. What have they done? What can you steal (ideas, not products)? What can you improve on? Is there anything they have done in a different field that is applicable to your problem?

Feedback

The aim here is not to copy, but to come up with something different, inspired by a combination of your problem and your competitors' actions. It is fine to reuse a concept or a feature that you feel you ought to have, but always be looking for that something extra that the opposition suggests, rather than duplication.

Outcome

Sometimes this technique will result in incremental improvements rather than major enhancements, but this is by no means always the case.

Variations

Try looking at totally different companies. Look for inspiration in the way they have handled a similar problem area. For example, a software company looking to package its products differently so they stand out on the shelf might want to look at a travel company, a manufacturer of washing powder and a car showroom.

Expertise: ✓✓
Direction setting: ✓
Idea generation: ✓✓✓✓
Problem solving: ✓✓✓
Fun: ✓✓

5.27 Behind it

Preparation:	None.
Running time:	10 minutes.
Resources:	None.
Teams:	Individual/team.

At the heart of every problem is a need. Very often this need occurs in many other circumstances. This technique expands thinking by looking at other areas where this need might occur.

The first thing to do is to identify the essential need in your problem, or at least one of the fundamentals. For instance, if you are trying to design seating, your essential need might be comfort, it might be style, or even fireproofing. Next think of three examples of this need in a different area. Taking style, we could think of clothes design, car design and the club scene as examples where style is important.

Finally, relate the external areas back to the problem. How can we apply clothes design to seating? An easy answer is to put whatever is happening on the catwalks on to our seats. From car design, we could focus on the centre of gravity – putting the driver at the heart of the seat. We could focus on streamlining. We could even take an inapplicable area of car design, like fuel efficiency, and ask how this could be applied. (An efficient build process for the seating would minimize effort in sitting and rising, or building a table into the seat would make human fuel intake easier.)

Feedback

Getting down to a lower level of need can be an effective way of bypassing some self-imposed obstacles. Looking outside is an established means of generating ideas; this technique helps to select the area of focus.

Outcome

Once the essential need is established, you will have little trouble applying the technique. You may have trouble identifying the central need – if so, settle for the most fundamental need you can find.

Variations

You could try combining needs. Given the seating example above, we could combine fashion design with old slippers (comfort) and try to find an area of stimulation in this. This is tougher to do and you might want to become experienced with the technique before doing so.

Expertise: ✓✓
Direction setting: ✓
Idea generation: ✓✓✓✓
Problem solving: ✓✓✓
Fun: ✓✓

5.28 Draw it

Preparation:	Get hold of materials.
Running time:	30 minutes.
Resources:	Artists' materials, magazines, glue, scissors, paper, etc.
Teams:	Individual/team.

The brain works in strange ways. The split brain theory suggests that half of your brain handles the logical, sequential, numerical thinking while the other half handles the holistic, artistic, imagery-based thinking. Whether you can locate the physical centres of these types of thought or not, it is certainly true that it feels different to think in different modes and that it is difficult to think holistically and sequentially at the same time. This technique is aimed at tapping into different ways of thinking by forcing you to express the problem and solutions in different ways.

Take a whole selection of artists' materials and produce an image of a world where your problem is solved or where your problem just doesn't exist. Having a selection of image-rich magazines is a bonus, because it means that those of us who write off our artistic ability can still produce an effective image.

Once you have produced the image look into it for clues to the solution to your problem. What do you see in there? What associations does it have for you? List these on to a flip chart.

Now take the words that you have generated and relate them back to your problem. What links can you make that take a step towards a solution?

Feedback

This technique is one of the most effective around at stretching thinking. In many ways, it combines some of the advantages of the random stimulation techniques with a probe into the darker recesses of your mind. If you have trouble with associations, see page 8 for guidance.

Outcome

Imagery proves useful in all sorts of circumstances for creating a new perspective and generating ideas.

Variations

This technique can be combined with others to increase the mental distance that you have to travel. For instance, try combining it with *Random word* (5.7) or *Shades* (5.19, eg, a pink, or matchbox, world in which your problem is solved, etc.)

Expertise:	✓✓
Direction setting:	✓
Idea generation:	✓✓✓
Problem solving:	✓✓✓
Fun:	✓✓

5.29 Touch me, feel me

Preparation:	None.
Running time:	10 minutes.
Resources:	A wide range of textures, boxes and blindfolds.
Teams:	Individual/team.

We have used all sorts of ways of stimulating people to move away from their problem in order to generate original solutions. This is one that works well if you are looking for very different solutions.

Collect together a wide range of textured materials. We have used different types of fabric, sandpaper, a bowl of jelly (Jell-O), wire wool, scouring pads, rubber gloves, sea shells, toys and small models. Place these objects into boxes in such a way that no one can see them. Blindfold some or all participants and ask them to feel the items. They must then give a running commentary of associations and metaphors that you record on to flip charts.

These associations are then used as material to relate back to your problem and to help to generate solutions. It is important that no one sees the objects during the exercise – neither the 'feelers' nor anyone responding to the spoken associations. Once the object is clearly visible it will lose the impact of the unknown.

Feedback

It can be difficult to persuade everybody to take part in this, so we suggest the option of having a few guinea pigs. There are some who will always be keen to try this sort of a challenge.

Outcome

This is a technique that we invented on the spur of the moment for a client who wanted to change the shape of an event as it was running. At the time we didn't have high hopes for it, but it turned out to be hugely successful at generating solutions to the problem that were radically different to other approaches. An advantage of this technique is that the resources can often be pulled together at short notice, as any working environment will have a good range of strange objects.

Variations

You can have the whole group experiencing the textures and making associations to work on later, or you can have a small subset of the group acting as guinea pigs.

Expertise: ✓✓
Direction setting: ✓
Idea generation: ✓✓✓✓
Problem solving: ✓✓✓
Fun: ✓✓✓

5.30 Evil genius

Preparation: None.
Running time: Five minutes.
Resources: None.
Teams: Individual/team.

There's a natural human tendency to blame problems on 'them' or imagine conspiracies where there aren't any. This technique makes use of this tendency. Whatever your problem, let's assume that there is an evil genius behind it. That your desired outcome would be true today, if it weren't for this malevolent monster getting in the way. To make this possible, you probably have to think about your problem in a slightly different way. If you wanted to cut costs, the evil genius could be both pushing up costs and thwarting any existing cost-cutting measures. If you want to come up with a fresh idea (although this is more a problem-solving technique) the evil genius could be making sure your competitors are one step ahead, and putting blockages in the way of making a new idea possible.

Think about the motivation of your nemesis. Why does he want things this way? Is there any way to satisfy him and still solve your problem? Is there any way of distracting him? Can you somehow trick him into solving the problem for you? Give it a try.

Feedback

This technique picks up on a long folk-story tradition of people thwarting giants or the devil in their attempts to make things unpleasant. By personifying the obstacles that cause your problem, you can see them in a different light, taking you towards a different solution.

Outcome

While there is no role play involved, this technique works best with people who are good at throwing themselves into character, as they have to imagine the machinations of the evil genius. It is surprising how often an intractable problem can be made more approachable by adding the human touch.

Variations

If using *Evil genius* in a group, you may like to have someone to play the Devil's Advocate, putting the case for the EG. If oo, thio peroon ohould be good at improvining and acting. You can use various alternatives of EG – the criminal mastermind, the mad scientist, the evil alien invaders, and so on.

Expertise:	✓✓✓
Direction setting:	✓
Idea generation:	✓
Problem solving:	✓✓✓✓
Fun:	✓✓✓

5.31 The game

Preparation:	None.
Running time:	10 to 15 minutes.
Resources:	None.
Teams:	Individual/team.

The makers of computer games have had to invent new and absorbing ways of interacting with the machine in order to satisfy their customers. If you were a business software developer you could learn from them. Then again, maybe we all could.

Imagine a computer adventure game. One of the characteristics is that the puzzles in the game have to have a high level of interest and absorption. Suppose that you were writing such a game and that the problem you face had to be solved by the players. How would you make your problem interesting? How would you describe it? How would you keep them interested? Finally, what hidden solution would you build in and where would it come from?

In designing your problem into a hypothetical game you are achieving two things: finding ways to make it interesting enough so that other people are prepared to help you to solve it, and gaining an understanding of the inner workings of your problem.

Take time after this exercise to examine what you have done for the lessons it might include. You might also go through an exercise of making associations with the game puzzle and forcing these associations back to the problem.

Feedback

We have set the expertise level high on this technique, not just because you need to know a fair amount about computer games to make it work, but because it can be a tricky one to facilitate a group through. If you are working on your own, this consideration doesn't arise.

Outcome

At the very least, this technique will generate an understanding of the workings of your problem. Beyond this, it will generate sets of ideas that will help you to engage others and will help you to move towards a solution.

Variations

Instead of a computer game, you could design your problem as a board game. This will lack some of the depth of the computer game, but gives you the opportunity to build in imagery that can act as a further source of inspiration.

Expertise:	✓✓✓✓
Direction setting:	✓
Idea generation:	✓✓✓
Problem solving:	✓✓✓
Fun:	✓✓✓

5.32 It's silly

Preparation:	None.
Running time:	10 minutes.
Resources:	Flip charts, paper and pens.
Teams:	Team.

First, spend four minutes on a conventional brainstorm. However, unlike a normal brainstorm, there is one crucial difference: only silly, unworkable, impractical or obscene suggestions are allowed. Ruthlessly weed out anything practical or sensible.

Then take a step back from the output of the brainstorming. How could you modify one of the silly suggestions to make it attractive? Could you change some aspect of it? Could you remove part of it or add to it to modify it? Could you turn it round on itself? Try to do this without watering down the suggestion too much.

Feedback

Traditional brainstorming is the weakest creativity technique, which is why it doesn't appear in this book. The problem is that it doesn't really break out of the current mode of thought and come at the problem from a totally different angle. However, by insisting that the original suggestions are outrageous, it is possible to ensure that conventional viewpoints are ignored. Don't allow excessive argument over what is or isn't silly. If there's any doubt, don't allow it.

Outcome

The ideas generated by this technique may have little connection with the actual problem, but the second stage will pull some around to a more realistic approach. This is, in effect, a variant of all the problem distortion techniques, where it is the solution that is being distorted rather than the problem.

Variations

It is possible to work on this one alone, but it is much better with a team of four to seven people. One variant is to split a group in two. The separated groups spend a few minutes generating impossible solutions, then swap solutions and try to make each other's solutions feasible. The initial 'crazy idea' session can also be done with individuals thinking up ideas alone, which are shared later (potentially anonymously on paper or electronically). This way there will be less inclination to be embarrassed by silly ideas. You can liven up the event by giving everyone water pistols with which to squirt anyone who writes up a sensible idea.

Expertise:	✓
Direction setting:	✓✓✓
Idea generation:	✓✓✓
Problem solving:	✓✓✓
Fun:	✓✓✓

5.33 **Been there before**

Preparation: None.
Running time: 10 minutes.
Resources: Paper and pens.
Teams: Individual/team.

In the popular film *Groundhog Day*, the hero relives the same day over and over again. Only he is aware of this. For everyone else, each morning is the first time around. By cleverly using the time available, the hero gains new skills that he needs to change things.

Assume that you are in the same sort of time loop. You can do almost anything, because next day you will wake up back in bed, with the previous day wiped out. You can take as long as you like to develop new skills and concepts – provided it can be done one day at a time, with only your memory to preserve what has happened from day to day. How could you attack your problem? What would you do? What lessons could you learn for the real world?

Feedback

Although in principle you could do almost anything, limit yourself to things you would be comfortable doing. Even if you knew you could get away with it, you might not rob a bank or kill someone. There's no real benefit from a solution that is in the form of 'go and get lots of money and throw it at the problem', unless the repeated day comes up with a new way of making money. Instead, you should look at the wider resources which could be built. If you are having trouble getting started, think through your general response to being stuck in a time loop first, before getting on to the problem.

Outcome

This is a very mixed technique. Sometimes it will come up with nothing at all, sometimes it will produce the exact solution you were looking for. It's one to try for five minutes, and if you aren't getting anywhere, try something else.

Variations

This one generally works best individually, but it is possible to work it with a team. If you have a team and have time, get everyone to do the exercise separately, share the results, then consider how you might change your approach if you were all sharing the experience of the repeated day simultaneously.

Expertise:	✓✓✓
Direction setting:	✓✓
Idea generation:	✓✓
Problem solving:	✓✓✓
Fun:	✓✓✓

5.34 Abattoir of sacred cows

Preparation:	None.
Running time:	10 to 20 minutes.
Resources:	Flip chart.
Teams:	Individual/team.

There are things about your company that have to be the way they are or that will not change as the result of a creativity session. These things will be ignored during the creation of ideas, because they are so fundamental that there is no point wasting time thinking about them. The risk that you, and all other companies, face is that there is a competitor out there, somewhere, who is willing to break those sacrosanct rules and, as a result, will take you to the cleaners.

Spend some time with the group thinking about the problem area and, in particular, the things around it that will always be the way they are. Now treat those aspects of the problem as sacred cows and wheel them into the abattoir. If these restrictions were removed, what obstacles would be removed with them? What problems would be caused by their removal? Now spend some time generating solutions to your problem in a world where this sort of restriction does not exist.

Feedback

You will find that the most difficult aspect of this technique is generating the initial list of sacred cows. In many businesses they are so much a part of the organization that they do not even appear consciously. One way to facilitate this is to start with a list of what we do around here; for instance, what do we wear, what time do we work, etc. Expand this list into a list of what others require us to do. Expand that into a list of what is required in the area of this problem.

Outcome

This technique works best in organizations that have a strong corporate culture. This is where the unwritten rules reside. In such an organization, it may offer real freedom to participants to generate fresh ideas.

Variations

If an outsider can be involved, they may spot your sacred cows better than you can.

Expertise: ✓✓
Direction setting: ✓✓
Idea generation: ✓✓✓✓
Problem solving: ✓✓✓✓
Fun: ✓✓✓

5.35 Size matters

Preparation:	None.
Running time:	10 minutes.
Resources:	Flip chart.
Teams:	Individual/team.

Many of the restrictions in your thinking about your company originate from its size. This technique and the next try to overcome that by changing your image of your company.

Once you have a clear problem statement, move on to discussing it in the context of the size of your company. If you were much bigger than all of your competitors and you dominated the industry, what solutions would then be available to you that are not now? What changes would have to occur in the company to allow such an industry domination? Is it these changes that would bring about the solution, or merely size?

Having discussed this aspect of size and having generated some solutions, try to bring them back to reality. What aspects of these solutions could your existing company put into place? If size is such an advantage, what techniques could you use to seem bigger than you are and thus achieve some of these benefits?

Feedback

This technique attacks one aspect of the assumptions that we make about our organizations. It isn't a particularly exciting one but can be effective.

Outcome

Most times when you use this technique it will be effective without being overwhelming. As with all techniques, it may just hit a nerve and cause the group to react strongly. If this is the case then you might find that it is much more impressive.

Variations

Instead of, or after, the 'much bigger' assumption, you could try looking at the implication of being much smaller than all your competitors – see *Lose the baggage* (5.36). Naturally, size is only one limiting factor and you could substitute any other for it. Be aware that there is a great deal that comes with company size, and that many of the other aspects that you might substitute for it could be encompassed within this dimension. Note that this is quite different from *Distortion* (5.2), where a dimension of the problem is varied. Here it is the company itself which is being changed – a very different prospect.

Expertise:	✓✓
Direction setting:	✓✓
Idea generation:	✓✓✓
Problem solving:	✓✓✓
Fun:	✓

5.36 Lose the baggage

Preparation:	None.
Running time:	10 minutes.
Resources:	Flip chart.
Teams:	Individual/team.

As with *Size matters* (5.35), this technique attempts to overcome the limitations on your thinking that is placed on you by the size of your company. This technique is particularly suited to large organizations.

Once you have a clear problem statement, move on to discussing it in the context of the size of your company. If you created a small start-up company to handle this problem, what solutions would be available to them that are not available to your current organization? What gets in the way that a start-up doesn't face? What would they be doing and how would they go about doing it?

Having discussed this aspect of size and generated some solutions, try to bring them back to reality. What aspects of these solutions could your existing company put into place? If being small is such an advantage, what techniques could you use to achieve some of these benefits?

Feedback

This technique attacks one aspect of the assumptions that we make about our organizations. Make sure that the participants think themselves as much as possible into a small company mentality. Any corporate thinking should be jumped on from a great height.

Outcome

Although very much an inversion of *Size matters* (5.35), this technique can generate much more energy and enthusiasm, because this reflects the nature of small companies. Accordingly, it will often be more successful, but not definitively so – be prepared to try both. One interesting possibility is that the solution actually is to create a start-up, either as a wholly independent company or a subsidiary. This catch-all solution is increasingly being employed to overcome otherwise insoluble problems.

Variations

As with *Size matters* (5.35), you could substitute another dimension. Be aware that there is a great deal that comes with company size, and that many of the other aspects you might substitute for it could be encompassed within this dimension.

Expertise: ✓✓
Direction setting: ✓✓
Idea generation: ✓✓✓
Problem solving: ✓✓✓✓
Fun: ✓✓

5.37 Auntie gravity

Preparation:	None.
Running time:	10 minutes.
Resources:	Flip chart.
Teams:	Individual / team.

Creativity techniques often attack the assumptions you make about the world. Many of these assumptions exist only in your head. This technique works on some of those that are real. It is particularly useful for product development.

First, think about a product. What capabilities does it need? What would be your absolutely ideal position? Now, take a step further. If you could overcome a fundamental law of physics, what would it be? For example, imagine that you could overcome gravity or you could develop a totally frictionless bearing. What difference could this make to your product? Next you need to make it real. Ideally, the way to do this would be to invent a way to overcome the law of physics, but it might be easier to look for other ways of getting the same benefits.

The idea behind this technique is that, once you have identified the benefits you are looking for, you will start to think of ways around the limitations and develop approaches which avoid breaking any physical laws.

Feedback

This is a technique that is harder to explain than it is to do. It really is quite easy, given a list of desired benefits, to think of all sorts of ways of making them happen. The tough part is freeing yourself up enough to get a meaningful list of benefits. The only reason for overcoming the physical law is to allow this freedom.

Outcome

Given a freewheeling start that allows for unlimited thinking as far as the physical laws are concerned, you will find that you generate a sizeable list of benefits attached to your ability to flout reality. This will lead to some useful ideas at the next stage where you develop those benefits within current physical reality.

Variations

You can miss out the stage of overcoming physical laws and move straight on to trying to list benefits, but there are dangers in this. The most likely outcome is that the benefits list that you generate is merely an extension of your current customer expectations, eg, the current product is only smaller, faster, pinker or with more output per channel.

Expertise:	✓✓
Direction setting:	✓✓✓
Idea generation:	✓✓✓✓
Problem solving:	✓✓✓
Fun:	✓✓

5.38 Long division

Preparation:	None.
Running time:	10 minutes.
Resources:	Flip chart.
Teams:	Individual/team.

Try to sum up the essence of your problem or requirement in a very few words – between two and four. For each of the words, think of a small number of words that describe key attributes of the words. Attach these to the initial words with lines, in mind map fashion. Now do the same again, producing attributes of attributes. For example, with a problem of 'how to increase European sales', the key words might be 'european' and 'sales'. European might have the attributes: large area, different languages, different food. Different food might have the attributes: spices, rich sauces, unusual ingredients. With all the elements filled in, pick and choose what takes your fancy. Browse over all the attributes at both levels. Make use of the sort of attribute link described in Chapter 2 (page 8) to tie back to possible solutions. Other solutions might emerge directly from the attributes.

Feedback

Don't worry about how silly the attributes may seem to other people. They don't have to be generally accepted or politically correct – just let them flow. It is important that you use the second level of attribute, as this often generates most positive effects.

Outcome

It is amazing how much depth is generated by reaching down two layers. One effect of the attribute approach is that it may uncover solutions that you had rejected subconsciously for being unsuitable that, with some modification, can be made practical.

Variations

The number of levels and quantity of words is arbitrary, although you must have two levels of attributes to get richness, but you don't want so many elements that the exercise becomes tedious. It is better if groups produce attributes individually, then share these or the linkages. Despite the name, this technique bears no relation to *Attributes* (5.22).

Expertise: ✓✓
Direction setting: ✓✓✓
Idea generation: ✓✓✓
Problem solving: ✓✓✓
Fun: ✓✓

5.39 It's only natural

Preparation:	None.
Running time:	10 to 15 minutes.
Resources:	Flip chart.
Teams:	Individual/team.

We have a lot to learn from nature. Many great ideas have been adapted from nature's solutions to problems.

Think about a natural analogy to your problem. If your office is too crowded, what overcrowding issues occur in nature? If you need a new springing mechanism, what springing mechanisms occur in nature? It need not be a one-to-one match. As with any analogy a very rough approximation is fine. The link between computer graphics and leaves may not be immediately obvious, but the development of fractals, the method of producing complex images from small mathematical 'seeds', was inspired by the way part of a leaf resembles the whole.

Having hit upon the analogy, look for ways that the natural world – geological, plant and animal – has found solutions to this problem. How can you adapt these to your problem? For instance, taking the overcrowding issue, bees swarm, some plants poison the soil around them, some animals fight to the death, some stop breeding. Any and all of these could be adapted to help to generate solutions for the overcrowded office (we particularly like the fighting to the death).

Feedback

The most important thing to remember is not to stop when you have a single example of nature doing what you need to do. Go for quantity. Jump around the whole span of nature.

Outcome

At first glance this would appear to be a technique that is particularly suited to product development. In practice, however, it works just as well with any problem area as long as you can find a good starting analogy.

Variations

Instead of working at finding an analogy, you could force fit one. Have a set of animals and plants and randomly assign one or two to each group as a forced analogy to this problem. Look for examples of them facing this or a similar problem and find ways that they would cope. If you are having trouble thinking of appropriate subjects, use an encyclopaedia of nature as a trigger.

Expertise: ✓✓
Direction setting: ✓✓✓
Idea generation: ✓✓✓✓
Problem solving: ✓✓✓✓
Fun: ✓✓

5.40 Location

Preparation:	Agreement with the venue.
Running time:	20 minutes.
Resources:	Flip chart (and muscles to carry it!).
Teams:	Team.

Look around you. There is plenty of stimulation for you to use in helping to solve your problem. This technique uses that fact.

If you are in a hotel, get agreement with the management about areas you can use. Take the group from area to area, with a flip chart stand, and note everything you see and every association it has. Crowd into bedrooms, bathrooms, seating areas, the garden, etc.

If you are in an office environment then you may need to take more time and move out of the office into the surrounding area. However you do it, you will need to cover many pieces of flip chart paper with observations and associations.

Back in the main meeting room take all of these flip charts and use them for stimulation in idea generation. What could a bed be in terms of your problem? What could a bottle of whisky be?

Feedback

A flip chart stand gets pretty heavy after a short while. You may need to line up volunteers to carry it for you or, perhaps, just take the paper without a stand. The more you can vary the areas you move between, the more stimulation this technique will provide.

Outcome

It is worth scheduling a significant amount of time for this activity. You will find that it is very rich in the ideas that it generates and the longer you spend, the richer it gets.

Variations

The more laughter you generate in this activity the more the results will stretch your thinking. How about getting everybody into or onto the bed together? How about miming different methods of shaving or cleaning your teeth in the bathroom? How about the whole group (including the women) trooping into the men's room (with some prior checking of course)?

Expertise: ✓✓
Direction setting: ✓✓✓
Idea generation: ✓✓✓✓
Problem solving: ✓✓✓
Fun: ✓✓✓

5.41 TV listings

Preparation:	Get TV listings and assign programmes to groups.
Running time:	20 minutes.
Resources:	Enough copies of today's TV listings for one per group.
Teams:	Individual/team.

This is a form of semi-random stimulation. Take copies of today's TV listings and assign programmes to the groups with which you will be working. Try to choose programmes such as soaps, films, situation comedies or dramas so that individuals within the groups will know a little of the types of storyline likely to develop and so that they have a chance to build the problem and resolution into them.

Have the groups write a plot for the programme that includes their problem and a resolution to it. How can it be resolved within the world of the programme? What resources are needed and how are they used? What characters play a key role? What characters get in the way and cause problems?

Having developed the storylines and shared them, bring them back to the real world and look for ways that this resolution could happen in your business. Who would the helpful characters be and how could you get them on side? Who would the obstacles be and how can you circumvent them or change their minds?

Feedback

This technique works well for problem solving and idea generation, but isn't great for new product development. The best problems to use it for are those involving people, as you can build people issues into TV programmes more easily than product or system issues.

Outcome

You are likely to find that this technique is enjoyed and appreciated by the group and that it is very effective at generating ideas. Try it out for different types of problems and see where it works for you.

Variations

If you have a lot of time and you want to enrich the exercise, you could get the groups to act out a small section of the plot. Be careful with this. Many groups will try to write something funny to act out. They don't need to, it will be funny anyway and most amateur humour gets pretty painful very quickly. Our advice would be to avoid attempts at humour, but to expect the results to be hilarious.

Expertise: ✓✓
Direction setting: ✓✓✓
Idea generation: ✓✓✓✓
Problem solving: ✓✓✓
Fun: ✓✓✓

5.42 Cacophony

Preparation: None.
Running time: Less than five minutes.
Resources: None.
Teams: Team (ideally quite large).

Get the group to focus on the problem and then give them all one or two minutes to list solutions – the wilder the better. Now have them all shout out their ideas, as loud as possible, at the same time. While shouting, they must also be aware of what's going on around them. You need to explain that the shouting out will create a wall of sound through which random snatches of other ideas will be heard. These random snatches will be the input for the next round.

Having done the shouting and listening, give the group another minute to write down any ideas that have come to them from this round. Have one more round of shouting and writing, and then collect what they have on their papers by taking input from the group on to flip charts. If the group is very large, split them for this stage to keep this activity short.

Feedback

One or two people in the group will hear the most absurd combinations of words and generate the best ideas. If you don't explain the random stimulation aspect at the beginning, some participants will feel that the whole thing is a waste of time and will refuse to play.

Outcome

This technique must be used as a very quick idea generator in conjunction with other techniques. It is not suitable alone because it will not generate a huge number of ideas, but will set you up quite well to use something else. With a large group and three rounds you may cover many pages of flip chart paper, but the ideas will be raw and undeveloped. Use this output as the input for a session of idea development, where appealing raw ideas are turned into something more usable.

Variations

Don't be tempted to spend too long on this even if it is going well. It really is a short, sharp shock tactic. The development of ideas generated could be done immediately after this technique, or could be kept until later when all raw ideas are developed together.

Expertise:	✓✓✓
Direction setting:	✓✓✓
Idea generation:	✓✓✓
Problem solving:	✓✓✓
Fun:	✓✓✓✓

5.43 Morphology

Preparation:	None.
Running time:	15 minutes.
Resources:	Flip chart and pen.
Teams:	Individual/team.

This technique uses the brain's ability to take something that doesn't fit in a particular place and force a connection. It is particularly useful for product development. We have used it for service development and we are sure that it could be used for idea generation and problem solving, but we haven't tried to adapt it to work there yet.

Define the product or service area you are trying to develop, write it up on a flip chart and then forget it. Next, take a completely dissimilar product or service and list all of the attributes of it that you can. What shape is it? What colour is it? What benefits does it offer the user? What controls does it have? How heavy is it? How portable is it? List anything and everything that you can use to describe it.

Now take each of those characteristics in turn and relate them back to the product or service you are trying to develop. For each of these characteristics, find customer benefits and start to think through how they could be made to happen.

Feedback

The toughest stage of this process is convincing a sceptical group that their canned soup product has anything to learn from a pocket camera. The only way to overcome this is to persuade them to trust you and to demonstrate that it works. You might want to try this one on your own beforehand, just to convince yourself of this.

Outcome

Given the right mix of dissimilar products, this technique will generate some truly original approaches. Make sure that they are not filtered out when you select ideas. It is too easy to stay within comfort zones at the selection and development phase.

Variations

You could preselect the product to be force fit or you could allow the group to select. With a little more time, you could use two very different products and combine their attributes.

Expertise:	✓✓✓
Direction setting:	✓✓
Idea generation:	✓✓✓✓
Problem solving:	✓✓
Fun:	✓✓✓

5.44 Talking pictures

Preparation:	None.
Running time:	20 minutes.
Resources:	One instant camera per group or a selection of bizarre photographs.
Teams:	Team.

Split the team into sub-groups and give each group an instant camera. Ask them to spend five minutes out of the room taking pictures that they can give to other groups as stimulation for idea generation. They may take pictures of bizarre objects or may take ordinary objects from an unusual angle. The more off-the-wall the pictures, the better.

Once back together, get each group to distribute their pictures to the other groups. Now in the sub-groups, they must take each of their pictures and list all associations that occur to them and then use these associations for idea generation.

At the end of the session, you can either collect all of the ideas together by writing them on to flip charts, or you can ask the groups to have listed their own and have these displayed for general perusal.

Feedback

This technique is the same as *Random picture* (5.8) in the way that it works. The advantage that it has is the element of challenge and competition that is thrown in by another group who have created the image, the humour generated when taking your own photos, and the extra energy that is always brought into an exercise by leaving the room and moving around.

Outcome

Talking pictures often generates more ideas of a better quality than *Random picture* for the reasons mentioned above. However, it does require more time and resources, and is only suitable for teams, so it does not replace that technique.

Variations

If you cannot get hold of enough cameras or film, you could either take the photographs yourself before the session, or you could ask for a single volunteer to take pictures for all of the groups in a tea break. However, doing so significantly reduces the advantages of the technique. Digital cameras, or video cameras and suitable playback equipment, could be substituted for instant cameras, if more readily available.

Expertise: ✓✓
Direction setting: ✓✓✓
Idea generation: ✓✓✓✓
Problem solving: ✓✓✓
Fun: ✓✓✓✓

5.45 Two words

Preparation:	None.
Running time:	15 minutes.
Resources:	Random word list.
Teams:	Individual/team.

This is a variant on *Random word* (5.7) that sounds as if it ought to work just the same, but in fact comes up with all sorts of synergistic possibilities that would not occur when using a simple random word. Choose not one, but two words from the random word list in Appendix 2 or another source – wherever they come from, ensure that they are both nouns.

Now think of the implications of combining these two words. Unlike the conventional random word, we are not looking for your personal associations with these words – instead, consider what new concepts arise from the combination. Think what you could do to solve your problem that is inspired by this combination. Consider both what links the two and what makes them different.

Feedback

The forced contrast of the two words generates a quite different set of associations than either word will individually. In a sense, this is one of the oldest forms of creativity – combining two unlike ideas to produce a third – but being used in a new way.

Outcome

Unlike *Random word*, this can be as good a technique for generating ideas as for solving problems. The possibilities arising from a dragon spittoon or a dolphin button (to name but two possibilities) are endless.

Variations

An alternative approach is to combine one of the adjectives from the *Shades* (5.19) list with one of the random words, coming up with, say a brown hole or a shiny freedom – but the stimulation provided by this combination is weaker. Where this technique is used in groups, get the individuals to develop their own thinking about the combined words first, or it will be too easy to be pushed towards a particular direction.

Expertise:	✓✓
Direction setting:	✓
Idea generation:	✓✓✓
Problem solving:	✓✓✓
Fun:	✓✓

5.46 Psychiatrist's couch

Preparation:	None.
Running time:	Five minutes.
Resources:	None.
Teams:	Individual.

To perform this exercise, imagine you are lying on a psychiatrist's couch. You are going to use free association. Pick out some key words in your 'how to' statement. (Not got a 'how to' statement? Get back to Chapter 4.) Take the first one and write down the word or short phrase it immediately makes you think of. Then take that word and do the same. Do this as quickly as you can without thinking. Go for at least five to seven words, then stop when you lose impetus. For example, your keyword might be 'profit'. This could generate a list: 'old testament', 'beard', 'wren', 'farthing', 'tarmac', 'plane', 'crash', 'stock market'. Perform the same exercise for the other key words you have.

Now write each association list alongside each other. Let your eyes move over the rows of words. What do they make you think of? What relevance does any combination of the words have to your problem?

Feedback

Like all techniques using association – in this case, a particularly free form of association – practice helps. See the advice in Chapter 2. Unlike a technique such as the *Level chain* (4.3), where there is structure in the list, here the words are apparently random. They will certainly appear so to another reader. But to you, each will have good reasons and rich associations. By following a set of links that your brain made automatically, yet combining several unconnected lists, you will have an excellent source of stimulation.

Outcome

There is usually plentiful output when using this technique, so it may be necessary to use one of the selection techniques at the end of this chapter as well. Because of the free nature of the association, you will also find wide variations in ideas from one individual.

Variations

While this is best run as an individual technique, there is nothing wrong with the members of a team all employing it at the same time, on the same 'what if' statement. However, they ought to build their association chains independently, both to avoid any analysis along the way, and to make sure they are as varied as possible.

Expertise:	✓✓
Direction setting:	✓✓✓
Idea generation:	✓✓✓✓
Problem solving:	✓✓✓✓
Fun:	✓✓

5.47 Mix and match

Preparation:	None.
Running time:	10 minutes.
Resources:	Trade magazines.
Teams:	Individual / team.

This technique needs a pile of trade magazines – the sort of business-specific publication you will find everywhere, from computing to plumbing. There should be at least three or four magazines, each from a different area of business. From each magazine extract the two or three stories about new products that are particularly outstanding. List in a few words what makes this product special (according to the article – you need know nothing about it). For example, a recent computer trade magazine has:

- a new network with a built in database, simplified management, better integration and good post office directory support;

- a power company branching out into water and gas expands its call centre;

- a university professor who has become a cyborg with a surgically implanted chip that opens doors, turns on his computer and reminds him about meetings.

Imagine combining these concepts with those from *Chicken Breeder's Monthly* and *Rubber Goods Today*. New product ideas will start flowing pretty quickly.

Feedback

Some ideas from this technique will be direct combinations of the products from the different fields. Others will be suggested by something – for example, the 'post office' in the network example has nothing to do with the Royal Mail, but it might generate an idea involving some aspect of that.

Outcome

The technique can be used to produce problem solutions by using the combined ideas from the trade magazines as pure random stimulation, but it is much more effective on new products, services and related ideas.

Variations

If you can't lay your hands on enough trade magazines, a quality newspaper will do, by combining aspects like business news, technology news, and so on, but it will be less effective. A group can be split into teams, each given a trade journal, who should then hunt out the key stories. They should then present the summaries (as above) back to the full group, who can work on the associations without the accompanying confusion of trade press jargon.

Expertise:	✓✓
Direction setting:	✓✓
Idea generation:	✓✓✓✓
Problem solving:	✓✓
Fun:	✓✓

5.48 Lost in translation

Preparation:　None.
Running time:　10 minutes.
Resources:　Internet access.
Teams:　Individual.

There are now facilities available on the internet which automatically translate from English to other languages and back again. At the time of writing, the best known of these are available at Google (**http://www.google.co.uk**) or Alta Vista (**http://www.altavista.com**) – but there are others available. First, write up a paragraph about your problem to include your 'how to' statement and a little about why you need to solve this problem and what it means to the company. Now pass this paragraph through a translator from English to another language. Retranslate back from the other language to English.

Read through the paragraph. The translation process will have introduced various misunderstandings and confusions into the text. Often the result is hilarious. Think of solving this newly stated problem. Think how aspects of the new statement could provide solutions for the original statement.

Feedback

Most techniques work by moving your viewpoint – this one moves the problem and sees what the outcome is. Translation is infamous for causing strife by changing meanings – here the worse the translation, the better.

Outcome

This technique is marginally better at problem solving than idea generation, but is quite capable of moving an existing idea in a totally unexpected direction provided the translation is bad enough.

Variations

You may like to try passing the paragraph back and forth between languages several times to see how it progresses. If the translation facility can handle translations between two other languages (eg, German to Portuguese), try a three-way translation, via two other languages, then back to English. There are also computer-based products with a similar functionality. One example is Power Translator Professional. These can be used as an alternative if there is no web access. However, they tend to be more effective, and will often only work between English and another language, making them less effective for managed confusion.

Expertise: ✓✓✓
Direction setting: ✓✓✓
Idea generation: ✓✓✓
Problem solving: ✓✓✓✓
Fun: ✓✓✓✓

5.49 They're winning

Preparation:	Scenario.
Running time:	10 minutes.
Resources:	None.
Teams:	Team.

This technique relies on deception, so can only be used with discretion. It depends on the fact that, given the knowledge that someone else has achieved a solution to a problem, most inventive people will come up with something, even if they had no idea previously. There have been famous (unintentional) examples of this in history, such as Charles with the gas balloon, and Bell with the telephone.

It does need a little preparation. Think of a likely scenario that would spur on the group. In the early days of the space race, the USA was kicked into action by the knowledge that the Russians had already got a satellite into orbit. You need a fictional equivalent of the Russians. It can be a competitor company, scientists in another country, whatever – but we 'know' that they have achieved a solution. Make up a few facts which are vague enough to avoid steering those participating, but add an element of truth. For instance, the man who thought it up is reported to be a heavy drinker, or the original prototype was much too heavy. Now sit back and let the group speculate. The results can be remarkable.

Feedback

If you want to use this technique more frequently, you can't keep up the deception, but you can get the participants to pretend that it's true. It works well with the pretence, but it works better with certainty – although you must let the participants down gently. This isn't a technique that works well for an individual – it is very dependent on the interplay of ideas. Note that this technique is also quite useful for justifying a creative solution that someone won't accept. 'Rumour has it, the competition is already doing this very successfully.'

Outcome

This isn't a technique for generating totally new ideas, but is excellent for cracking stubborn problems.

Variations

This technique is effectively reverse engineering a non-existent solution. A variant is to reverse engineer a real solution to a rather different problem and use this as input to the process.

Expertise: ✓✓
Direction setting: ✓✓
Idea generation: ✓
Problem solving: ✓✓✓
Fun: ✓✓

5.50 The £100 bid

Preparation:	None.
Running time:	Five minutes.
Resources:	None.
Teams:	Team.

The remaining techniques in this section are not about creating ideas or solutions to problems, but are about selecting from them.

When you have had a particularly successful session, you will have walls covered with raw ideas and you will have developed some of those into more complete solutions that are suitable for implementation. How do you select from this mess? The simplest way is to simply say, 'Choose' and then see what happens. A more democratic way of choosing is using a £100 bid.

Give everyone in the group a notional £100 and instruct them that they can spread this over the ideas in any way they choose. They can put all £100 on to one idea, they can split it over two or they could even put £1 on to 100 different ideas.

Once everybody has had an opportunity to bid, add up the money attached to each idea and the idea with the highest amount is taken forward.

Feedback

This is a relatively fast and painless way of selecting from a list. It has an advantage over the slightly easier process of putting stickers next to your favourites because it allows more precise weighting. If you feel very strongly about an idea, you can make that feeling have an effect. If you are really not too worried, then this will also be reflected in your votes.

Outcome

Having used this technique, groups are almost always satisfied with the decision. Sometimes there is a plea to allow one more idea past the hurdle and, depending upon the next stage, this is rarely a problem. Obviously, if you have too many pleas for additional ideas to sneak through then you are diluting the effect of having made a selection.

Variations

The amount given for distribution is somewhat arbitrary. We have found that £100 allows for enough variations to avoid limiting people, but is faster than, say, £1,000. Alternatively give each participant five coloured stickers as their 'cash'.

Expertise:	✓✓
Direction setting:	✓✓✓✓
Idea generation:	✓
Problem solving:	✓
Fun:	✓

5.51 SWOT

Preparation:	None.
Running time:	15 minutes (or significantly more, depending upon approach).
Resources:	None.
Teams:	Individual/team.

This technique is another one for selection, ideally where there is a relatively small range of options to choose between. Most people will have come across it in other circumstances, but not usually as a way of selecting ideas.

For those who have not used the technique, *SWOT* stands for Strengths, Weaknesses, Opportunities and Threats. The results are normally expressed as a quadrant on one sheet of paper for easy viewing.

Take each idea in turn and analyse the strengths, weaknesses, opportunities and threats attached to each of those that you might take forward. Use the results to select those that offer you the best combination of maximizing the positives and minimizing the negatives. In some circumstances, you might be trying to develop a really safe idea. This would mean minimizing negatives. In some circumstances you might be trying to push your organization further; in this case you would look to maximize the positives.

Naturally, the degree of analysis that you go into will depend upon the importance of this selection. This does not involve judging the importance of the final idea, but the importance of being absolutely right in the selection at this stage.

Feedback

The advantage of this technique is that most people in a group have used it before and settle quite comfortably into using it for idea selection. It can, however, be very time consuming, particularly if you develop the analysis to a very detailed level.

Outcome

It may take time, but you will have a selection that everyone feels is detailed and complete.

Variations

If you are working with a group that is large enough to split into teams, then you can divide the ideas amongst them for the initial SWOT analysis and they can feed back their results.

Expertise:	✓✓✓
Direction setting:	✓✓✓✓
Idea generation:	✓
Problem solving:	✓
Fun:	✓

5.52 Option evaluation

Preparation:	None.
Running time:	10 minutes.
Resources:	None.
Teams:	Individual/team.

Another special technique for sorting out a range of ideas, *Option evaluation* provides an alternative to *SWOT* (5.51). Take two minutes to devise a set of criteria by which you will decide between ideas. General criteria might be appeal, originality, pizzazz and practicality. Others might be timescale, resources required, cost and so on.

Now draw up a grid. Down the side, list the ideas. If you've more than five, whittle them down quickly to five by gut feel alone – having too many options in an evaluation simply floods you with data. Across the top, list the criteria. Now rate the ideas on your criteria. Use a scale that's appropriate to the problem – it might be high, medium and low, or 0 to 10. Certain criteria might be a decisive factor – an idea is only usable if it has this factor – for these you can use a tick (check) box.

If there isn't an obvious winner, you can add up the scores and use these as a guide.

Feedback

However you reach your output, bear in mind that this approach only gives a guide – you need to take account of your gut feel as well. When looking for a creative solution, it is probably worth giving more weight to the 'creative' criteria (like originality, pizzazz) than the 'everyday' criteria (like practicality). An idea can be made more practical – it's much harder to make it more creative.

Outcome

When you have a range of good ideas, but aren't certain with which to go forward, this is a great way of homing in on a particular approach.

Variations

One of the benefits of using *Option evaluation* with a group is that it forces the members to make the reasoning behind their preferences explicit. That way they are much more likely to agree on a course of action (even if it bears no resemblance to the 'best' idea according to the basic ratings made in option evaluation). There are software packages available to help with *Option evaluation*. See the Creativity Unleashed website in Chapter 6 for information.

Expertise:	✓
Direction setting:	✓✓✓
Idea generation:	✓
Problem solving:	✓
Fun:	✓

5.53 Signposts

Preparation:	None.
Running time:	Five minutes.
Resources:	None.
Teams:	Individual / team.

This technique and *Hazard markers* (5.54) follow on from the previous three but, rather than a pure selection technique, *Signposts* can be used either to make it clearer which idea in a list to choose, or to enhance an idea that has already been selected.

For selection, the technique itself is mind-bogglingly simple. You merely list all of the things about the idea that are positive. Yes, that's it. The next question is, why would you bother?

Most people take evaluation to mean a negative criticism. When you ask for an open evaluation of ideas, you tend to get a whole list of negatives. Then you find that proponents of particular ideas start defending them against attack and rational thought flies out of the window.

Structuring the evaluation into listing positives and listing negatives separately makes the whole process less emotive, less confrontational and more effective. It is generally also a good idea to list positives before listing the negatives, because then there is less defensiveness about the negatives.

If you are using *Signposts* to refine rather than to select, once you have stated the positives, go on to say how you can make these good points even better.

Feedback

This takes very little time and is a necessary stage of the process. Don't drop it.

Outcome

Signposts, followed by *Hazard markers*, gives a much clearer picture of where the ideas stand and can actually lead to further development.

Variations

When evaluating a collection of ideas you can either take each idea and list positives and negatives, or take all of the ideas through *Signposts* first and then go through *Hazard markers* with them all. Usually, with two or three ideas, we find that the second approach works; with more than this it makes sense to stick to an idea at a time and go through both halves. Evaluation can be done in the whole group or in smaller teams with feedback.

Expertise: ✓
Direction setting: ✓✓✓
Idea generation: ✓
Problem solving: ✓
Fun: ✓✓

5.54 Hazard markers

Preparation:	None.
Running time:	Five minutes.
Resources:	None.
Teams:	Individual / team.

In some ways, *Hazard markers* has already been introduced in *Signposts* (5.53). This is the negative stage where the previous one was positive. In other words, for this technique you list all of the negatives associated with the idea.

Having done this, you have a decision to make. What are you going to do about it? Decide how complete and how positive you need the developed ideas to be, and then you can either accept the negatives you have listed or do something about them.

If you are going to do something about them you can either attack them directly or, given time and an idea that warrants it, you could go back to problem solving techniques using this negative as the problem.

This starts to sound like an infinite loop. You will always be able to find negatives for any idea and, if you then go back to problem solving, you will continue around and around and around. That is why the decision about the completeness of the answer is important. This helps you to decide where to stop the loop.

Feedback

Like *Signposts*, this takes very little time and is a necessary stage of the process. Don't drop it.

Outcome

Hazard markers lets you understand what further development is still needed to make your idea work.

Variations

When evaluating a collection of ideas, you can either take each idea and list positives and negatives or take all of the ideas through *Signposts* first and then go through *Hazard markers* with them all. Usually, with two or three ideas we find that the second approach works; with more than this it makes sense to stick to an idea at a time and go through both halves. Evaluation can be done in the whole group or in smaller teams with feedback.

Expertise:	✓
Direction setting:	✓✓✓
Idea generation:	✓
Problem solving:	✓
Fun:	✓✓

6

Other sources

There's more

Instant Creativity gives you all you need to bring out the spark of innovation, but there are plenty more sources of instant creativity, plus more that can be done with extra time. This short chapter is a resource kit for going beyond *Instant Creativity*.

Reading up

Creativity is a broad subject, which can be found as much on the psychology shelves as the business section. These recommendations focus on the practical side of the discipline. If you would like to explore more of the theory, check the Creativity Unleashed online bookshop at **http://www.cul. co.uk/books**, which provides plenty of information and direct buying links to the biggest online bookshops in the US and the UK. It's also worth checking there for more up-to-date references, and for books which are hard to get hold of in the UK.

More depth

Creativity works at more than one level. To address a major project, or to instil a creative culture in a company, requires a very different approach. These books give a broader view of creativity, but keep the entirely practical approach.

Brian Clegg, *Creativity and Innovation for Managers*, Butterworth Heinemann, 1999
An overview for the busy manager, showing the need for creativity, where it came from as a management discipline, how it is applied and how to make it work in a company. Puts creativity alongside other business techniques, and provides an agenda for introducing corporate innovation.

Paul Birch and Brian Clegg, *Imagination Engineering*, Pitman Publishing, 1999
A toolkit for business creativity, providing a practical but enjoyable guide to making creativity work. Introduces a four-stage process for business creativity, equally applicable for a five-minute session or a week concentrating on a single problem. Plenty of depth, but fun, too.

Tony and Barry Buzan, *The Mind Map Book*, BBC Books, 2003
A beautifully illustrated guide to the use of mind maps to take notes, structure ideas and aid memory. Written by Tony Buzan, the developer of the mind map concept, with his brother.

Edward de Bono, *Serious Creativity*, HarperCollins, 1996
A wide-ranging book from the best-known UK creativity guru. De Bono invented the term 'lateral thinking', and here he explores the benefits of creativity and describes his personally preferred techniques. Quite a dry book, but pulls together all de Bono's key work on the subject.

Roger von Oech, *A Whack on the Side of the Head*, Fine Communications, 2002
In total contrast to de Bono, von Oech's laid-back Californian style attacks the blockers to creativity in an enjoyable way. Sometimes feels more like a humour book than a management text, but none the worse for this, and there's a serious message under the gloss.

Something completely different

Sometimes the best way of enhancing creativity is to read something from a totally different field to your problem area. When you return to the problem, you will be refreshed and see things in a different light. Almost anything will do, but we particularly recommend business bios – those fascinating books that combine the story of a business and real people – business humour and science fiction for a totally different view. Even if you wouldn't normally read science fiction, try it as a creative catalyst. All three subjects are covered in the Creativity Unleashed online bookshop, **http://www.cul. co.uk/books**.

E-creativity

The internet is now a prime source of creativity, both as a stimulator and as a source of extra information. In the techniques we have mentioned a number of possibilities for using everyday computer software for creativity – there are also specialist packages available that are specifically designed to support creativity techniques; again the internet is probably the best source.

Instant creativity

For instant creativity techniques online and more information on creativity in general, try the website:

http://www.cul.co.uk/creative

Another way to get an instant creative hit is to use the web itself as a stimulus. Try randomly surfing for five minutes, or use one of the 'cool site' or 'site of the day' features to find something interesting. This can then be used as a simple distraction, or like *Random picture* (see techniques 5.8).

Creativity software

Try these sites, which generally have free software or shareware on offer:

http://www.cul.co.uk/software – general creativity software
http://www.coco.co.uk – VisiMap idea mapping software
http://www.mindtools.com – mind development software
http://mindjet.com – mind mapping software

Training, consulting and facilitating

An awful lot can be done with a book like this, or with the more in-depth books listed above, but it is often necessary to go further. A number of companies offer training in creativity techniques, direct consulting using creativity and facilitation of creativity sessions. Our own companies' details are provided below – try the links section of the Creativity Unleashed website at **http://www.cul.co.uk/links** or putting 'creativity' into a search engine on the web to find more.

Creativity Unleashed Limited
The Thicket, Upper Wanborough, Wiltshire SN4 0DQ
Website: **http://www.cul.co.uk**
E-mail: info@cul.co.uk
Telephone/Fax: 01793 791393

Visionjuice Ltd
2 St John's Road, Taunton, Somerset TA1 4AZ
Website: **http://www.visionjuice.com**
E-mail: paul@visionjuice.com
Telephone: 01823 321731

Appendix 1
The Selector

The Random Selector

Take a watch with a second hand and note the number the second hand is pointing at now. Take that number technique from the list of 60 below. These are almost all from Chapter 5, but exclude the techniques that are designed to help to select or refine ideas, and include several from Chapter 4, which are equally effective at defining the question and producing the answer.

No.	Ref.	Title	No.	Ref.	Title
1	4.3	The level chain	22	5.11	On this day
2	4.6	Do nothing	23	5.12	Cool site
3	4.7	Shorts	24	5.13	Headlines
4	4.8	Adventure	25	5.14	Quotations
5	4.9	Outside in	26	5.15	Squirrel box
6	4.12	Thesaurus	27	5.16	Set it to music
7	4.16	Army of a thousand	28	5.17	Da Vinci scribbles
8	4.17	Solve a different problem	29	5.18	Inside view
9	4.19	Mud slinging	30	5.19	Shades
10	4.20	Questions race	31	5.20	Problem perfect
11	4.21	Whiteboard	32	5.21	Frontiers
12	5.1	Challenging assumptions	33	5.22	Attributes
13	5.2	Distortion	34	5.23	Kid's play
14	5.3	Reversal	35	5.24	Components
15	5.4	Fantasy	36	5.25	Substitutes
16	5.5	Someone else's view	37	5.26	It's a steal
17	5.6	Metaphor	38	5.27	Behind it
18	5.7	Random word	39	5.28	Draw it
19	5.8	Random picture	40	5.29	Touch me, feel me
20	5.9	Found objects	41	5.30	Evil genius
21	5.10	Nonsense sentence	42	5.31	The game

No.	Ref.	Title		No.	Ref.	Title
43	5.32	It's silly		52	5.41	TV listings
44	5.33	Been there before		53	5.42	Cacophony
45	5.34	Abattoir of sacred cows		54	5.43	Morphology
46	5.35	Size matters		55	5.44	Talking pictures
47	5.36	Lose the baggage		56	5.45	Two words
48	5.37	Auntie gravity		57	5.46	Psychiatrist's couch
49	5.38	Long division		58	5.47	Mix and match
50	5.39	It's only natural		59	5.48	Lost in translation
51	5.40	Location		60	5.49	They're winning

Techniques in timing order

This table sorts the techniques by the suggested timings. Those at the top take the longest, those towards the bottom are the quickest.

No	Technique		No	Technique
	30 minutes		5.6	Metaphor
5.26	It's a steal		5.7	Random word
5.28	Draw it		5.8	Random picture
	20 minutes		5.10	Nonsense sentence
4.8	Adventure		5.11	On this day
5.9	Found objects		5.12	Cool site
5.40	Location		5.13	Headlines
5.41	TV listings		5.14	Quotations
5.44	Talking pictures		5.15	Squirrel box
	15 minutes		5.16	Set it to music
5.1	Challenging assumptions		5.17	Da Vinci scribbles
5.2	Distortion		5.18	Inside view
5.3	Reversal		5.19	Shades
5.5	Someone else's view		5.22	Attributes
5.34	Abattoir of sacred cows		5.23	Kid's play
5.43	Morphology		5.24	Components
5.45	Two words		5.25	Substitute
5.51	SWOT		5.27	Behind it
	10 minutes		5.29	Touch me, feel me
4.4	Aerial survey		5.31	The game
4.7	Shorts		5.32	It's silly
4.9	Outside in		5.33	Been there before
4.10	Up and down		5.35	Size matters
4.11	Time slices		5.36	Lose the baggage
4.13	Crystal ball		5.37	Auntie gravity
4.14	Web wandering		5.38	Long division
4.17	Solve a different problem		5.39	It's only natural
4.19	Mud slinging		5.47	Mix and match
5.4	Fantasy		5.48	Lost in translation

5.49	They're winning	4.18	Restatement
5.52	Option evaluation	4.20	Questions race
	5 minutes	4.21	Whiteboard
4.1	Compass	5.20	Problem perfect
4.2	Obstacle map	5.21	Frontiers
4.3	The level chain	5.30	Evil genius
4.5	Destination	5.42	Cacophony
4.6	Do nothing	5.46	Psychiatrist's couch
4.12	Thesaurus	5.50	The £100 bid
4.15	Excellence	5.53	Signposts
4.16	Army of a thousand	5.54	Hazard markers

Techniques in expertise order

This table sorts the techniques by the expertise ratings attached to each. Those at the top have the highest rating, those at the bottom the lowest.

No	Technique	No	Technique
	✓✓✓✓	4.17	Solve a different problem
5.31	The game	4.20	Questions race
	✓✓✓	4.21	Whiteboard
4.4	Aerial survey	5.1	Challenging assumptions
4.14	Web wandering	5.2	Distortion
5.4	Fantasy	5.3	Reversal
5.6	Metaphor	5.5	Someone else's view
5.20	Problem perfect	5.7	Random word
5.21	Frontiers	5.8	Random picture
5.22	Attributes	5.9	Found objects
5.30	Evil genius	5.10	Nonsense sentence
5.33	Been there before	5.11	On this day
5.42	Cacophony	5.12	Cool site
5.43	Morphology	5.13	Headlines
5.48	Lost in translation	5.15	Squirrel box
5.51	SWOT	5.17	Da Vinci scribbles
5.55	Second best solution	5.18	Inside view
	✓✓	5.19	Shades
4.3	The level chain	5.26	It's a steal
4.7	Shorts	5.27	Behind it
4.8	Adventure	5.28	Draw it
4.10	Up and down	5.29	Touch me, feel me
4.11	Time slices	5.34	Abattoir of sacred cows
4.12	Thesaurus	5.35	Size matters
4.13	Crystal ball	5.36	Lose the baggage
4.15	Excellence	5.37	Auntie gravity
4.16	Army of a thousand	5.38	Long division

5.39	It's only natural	4.6	Do nothing
5.40	Location	4.9	Outside in
5.41	TV listings	4.18	Restatement
5.44	Talking pictures	4.19	Mud slinging
5.45	Two words	5.14	Quotations
5.46	Psychiatrist's couch	5.16	Set it to music
5.47	Mix and match	5.23	Kid's play
5.49	They're winning	5.24	Components
5.50	The £100 bid	5.25	Substitute
	✓	5.32	It's silly
4.1	Compass	5.52	Option evaluation
4.2	Obstacle map	5.53	Signposts
4.5	Destination	5.54	Hazard markers

Techniques in direction setting order

This table sorts the techniques by the direction setting ratings attached to each. Those at the top have the highest rating, those at the bottom the lowest.

No	Technique	No	Technique
	✓✓✓✓	5.11	On this day
4.1	Compass	5.14	Quotations
4.2	Obstacle map	5.20	Problem perfect
4.3	The level chain	5.21	Frontiers
4.4	Aerial survey	5.22	Attributes
4.6	Do nothing	5.32	It's silly
4.10	Up and down	5.37	Auntie gravity
4.14	Web wandering	5.38	Long division
4.15	Excellence	5.39	It's only natural
4.19	Mud slinging	5.40	Location
5.50	The £100 bid	5.41	TV listings
5.51	SWOT	5.42	Cacophony
5.52	Option evaluation	5.44	Talking pictures
	✓✓✓	5.46	Psychiatrist's couch
4.5	Destination	5.48	Lost in translation
4.7	Shorts	5.53	Signposts
4.8	Adventure	5.54	Hazard markers
4.9	Outside in		✓✓
4.11	Time slices	5.1	Challenging assumptions
4.12	Thesaurus	5.2	Distortion
4.13	Crystal ball	5.3	Reversal
4.16	Army of a thousand	5.4	Fantasy
4.17	Solve a different problem	5.5	Someone else's view
4.18	Restatement	5.6	Metaphor
4.20	Questions race	5.7	Random word
4.21	Whiteboard	5.8	Random picture

5.9	Found objects	5.35	Size matters
5.10	Nonsense sentence	5.36	Lose the baggage
5.12	Cool site	5.43	Morphology
5.13	Headlines	5.47	Mix and match
5.15	Squirrel box	5.49	They're winning
5.16	Set it to music		✓
5.17	Da Vinci scribbles	5.26	It's a steal
5.18	Inside view	5.27	Behind it
5.19	Shades	5.28	Draw it
5.23	Kid's play	5.29	Touch me, feel me
5.24	Components	5.30	Evil genius
5.25	Substitute	5.31	The game
5.33	Been there before	5.45	Two words
5.34	Abattoir of sacred cows		

Techniques in idea generation order

This table sorts the techniques by the idea generation ratings attached to each. Those at the top have the highest rating, those at the bottom the lowest.

No	Technique	No	Technique
	✓✓✓✓	5.41	TV listings
4.3	The level chain	5.43	Morphology
5.1	Challenging assumptions	5.44	Talking pictures
5.2	Distortion	5.46	Psychiatrist's couch
5.6	Metaphor	5.47	Mix and match
5.7	Random word		✓✓✓
5.8	Random picture	4.12	Thesaurus
5.9	Found objects	4.19	Mud slinging
5.12	Cool site	5.4	Fantasy
5.14	Quotations	5.5	Someone else's view
5.15	Squirrel box	5.10	Nonsense sentence
5.16	Set it to music	5.13	Headlines
5.17	Da Vinci scribbles	5.19	Shades
5.18	Inside view	5.22	Attributes
5.23	Kid's play	5.28	Draw it
5.25	Substitute	5.31	The game
5.26	It's a steal	5.32	It's silly
5.27	Behind it	5.35	Size matters
5.29	Touch me, feel me	5.36	Lose the baggage
5.34	Abattoir of sacred cows	5.38	Long division
5.37	Auntie gravity	5.42	Cacophony
5.39	It's only natural	5.45	Two words
5.40	Location	5.48	Lost in translation

	✓✓		4.2	Obstacle map
4.7	Shorts		4.4	Aerial survey
4.8	Adventure		4.5	Destination
4.9	Outside in		4.6	Do nothing
4.10	Up and down		4.11	Time slices
4.14	Web wandering		4.13	Crystal ball
4.16	Army of a thousand		4.15	Excellence
4.17	Solve a different problem		4.18	Restatement
4.20	Questions race		5.3	Reversal
4.21	Whiteboard		5.30	Evil genius
5.11	On this day		5.49	They're winning
5.20	Problem perfect		5.50	The £100 bid
5.21	Frontiers		5.51	SWOT
5.24	Components		5.52	Option evaluation
5.33	Been there before		5.53	Signposts
	✓		5.54	Hazard markers
4.1	Compass			

Techniques in problem solving order

This table sorts the techniques by the problem solving ratings attached to each. Those at the top have the highest rating, those at the bottom the lowest.

No	Technique		No	Technique
	✓✓✓✓		5.48	Lost in translation
5.1	Challenging assumptions			✓✓✓
5.3	Reversal		4.6	Do nothing
5.5	Someone else's view		4.17	Solve a different problem
5.6	Metaphor		5.2	Distortion
5.7	Random word		5.4	Fantasy
5.9	Found objects		5.8	Random picture
5.11	On this day		5.10	Nonsense sentence
5.12	Cool site		5.13	Headlines
5.14	Quotations		5.16	Set it to music
5.15	Squirrel box		5.17	Da Vinci scribbles
5.18	Inside view		5.20	Problem perfect
5.19	Shades		5.22	Attributes
5.21	Frontiers		5.26	It's a steal
5.23	Kid's play		5.27	Behind it
5.24	Components		5.28	Draw it
5.25	Substitute		5.29	Touch me, feel me
5.30	Evil genius		5.31	The game
5.34	Abattoir of sacred cows		5.32	It's silly
5.36	Lose the baggage		5.33	Been there before
5.39	It's only natural		5.35	Size matters
5.46	Psychiatrist's couch		5.37	Auntie gravity

5.38	Long division	5.43	Morphology
5.40	Location	5.47	Mix and match
5.41	TV listings		✓
5.42	Cacophony	4.1	Compass
5.44	Talking pictures	4.2	Obstacle map
5.45	Two words	4.3	The level chain
5.49	They're winning	4.4	Aerial survey
	✓✓	4.5	Destination
4.7	Shorts	4.13	Crystal ball
4.8	Adventure	4.14	Web wandering
4.9	Outside in	4.15	Excellence
4.10	Up and down	4.19	Mud slinging
4.11	Time slices	5.50	The £100 bid
4.12	Thesaurus	5.51	SWOT
4.16	Army of a thousand	5.52	Option analysis
4.18	Restatement	5.53	Signposts
4.20	Questions race	5.54	Hazard markers
4.21	Whiteboard		

Techniques in fun order

This table sorts the techniques by the fun ratings attached to each. Those at the top have the highest rating, those at the bottom the lowest.

No	Technique	No	Technique
	✓✓✓✓	5.21	Frontiers
4.8	Adventure	5.23	Kid's play
4.19	Mud slinging	5.29	Touch me, feel me
5.9	Found objects	5.30	Evil genius
5.42	Cacophony	5.31	The game
5.44	Talking pictures	5.32	It's silly
5.48	Lost in translation	5.33	Been there before
	✓✓✓	5.34	Abattoir of sacred cows
4.3	The level chain	5.40	Location
4.7	Shorts	5.41	TV listings
4.14	Web wandering	5.43	Morphology
4.17	Solve a different problem		✓✓
4.20	Questions race	4.1	Compass
5.3	Reversal	4.6	Do nothing
5.5	Someone else's view	4.9	Outside in
5.8	Random picture	4.10	Up and down
5.11	On this day	4.11	Time slices
5.12	Cool site	4.12	Thesaurus
5.14	Quotations	4.13	Crystal ball
5.15	Squirrel box	4.15	Excellence
5.18	Inside view	4.16	Army of a thousand
5.19	Shades	4.18	Restatement

Appendix 2
Lists for techniques

5.5 Someone else's view

Feel free to invent your own persona, but this list will give you a prompt if you need some in a hurry. Don't try to select a person to fit the problem, pick one at random. The list has 60 names to facilitate the method popularized by Edward de Bono of choosing an item by checking the second hand of a watch.

1	Hercule Poirot	23	Attila the Hun
2	Sherlock Holmes	24	A prostitute in Paris
3	A Rabbi	25	Queen Elizabeth the First
4	A Roman Catholic priest	26	A beggar in Bombay
5	A poet	27	Superman
6	A trapeze artist	28	The Pope
7	A circus clown	29	A New York cab driver
8	A surgeon	30	Donald Duck
9	A nasturtium	31	A blind person
10	George Washington	32	Paul McCartney
11	Groucho Marx	33	A court jester
12	Karl Marx	34	An ant
13	Beethoven	35	Billy the Kid
14	A computer programmer	36	Count Dracula
15	Robin Hood	37	Winston Churchill
16	A mass murderer	38	A martian
17	A pet rabbit	39	A Star Trek character
18	The President of the United States	40	Queen Victoria
19	Marilyn Monroe	41	Jane Austen
20	A plumber	42	Oscar Wilde
21	A Roman centurion	43	An X-Files character
22	William Shakespeare	44	A World War 2 fighter pilot
		45	A nurse

46	Winnie the Pooh	54	Hercules
47	Alice (in Wonderland)	55	James Bond
48	Bart Simpson	56	A stage magician
49	Charlie Chaplin	57	A druid
50	A bee keeper	58	Cyrano de Bergerac
51	Bill Gates	59	A mermaid
52	Margaret Thatcher	60	Joan of Arc
53	The Phantom of the Opera		

5.7 Random word and 5.45 Two words

Feel free to invent your own words, but this list will give you a prompt if you need some in a hurry. Don't try to select a word to fit the problem, pick one at random. The list has 60 items to facilitate the method popularized by Edward de Bono of choosing an item by checking the second hand of a watch.

1	Cat	31	Teeth
2	Gold bar	32	Breakfast
3	Desk	33	Map
4	Stopwatch	34	Glue
5	Fire	35	Bark
6	Forest glade	36	Bikini
7	City	37	Scar
8	Autumn	38	Bed
9	Dolls' house	39	Box
10	Dragon	40	Music
11	Magic carpet	41	Wallpaper
12	War	42	Missing
13	Peace	43	Photograph
14	Scales	44	Wind chimes
15	Cigar	45	Hole
16	Hat	46	Share
17	Chewing gum	47	Telephone
18	Spittoon	48	Cartoon
19	Rainbow	49	Baby
20	Dolphin	50	Sunset
21	Fence	51	Telescope
22	Pain	52	Silence
23	Button	53	School
24	Mirror	54	T-shirt
25	Compact disc	55	Freedom
26	Air freshener	56	Road
27	Happiness	57	Sea
28	Flower	58	Sweat
29	Christmas	59	Monk
30	Swan	60	Shelf

5.10 Nonsense sentence

It is harder to invent your own nonsense sentences than it is to invent characters or random words. We have written a program to assist in this and used this to generate the list below. The list has 60 items to facilitate the method popularized by Edward de Bono of choosing an item by checking the second hand of a watch.

1   A bikly light switch for use as camouflage
2   The first ever bronze chairve displayed on a postage stamp
3   An Australian schiefe with a broken top
4   A slow jiafe for slowing a speeding car
5   A fneecly kitchen appliance
6   An African tribal psih for tangle free hair
7   A skaiping priatre
8   A druply thient
9   A slaerming sliascr
10 A ferking onion
11 A smelly zish
12 A rirking keyboard
13 An enormous zoos which is reliable to a depth of thirty fathoms
14 A vugh with which to grairt a steism
15 A zuning elephant
16 A quebly banana
17 A quiank with which to creiro a zeri
18 A dreeply xourp
19 A gilded knieny belonging to a child
20 A cabra with which to klarf a nouw
21 A placrly light switch
22 The only absolutely square skeiro
23 A sunken share for use on the beach
24 A piarsly waste bin for quieting your noisy neighbours
25 A tall ciapre
26 A sclecly toupee
27 A leirply krij

28 A bronze seed for use by the army
29 A crooschly plug chewed by a dog
30 A grabyly beach ball
31 A geping extension socket
32 A keeroly desk
33 A badly repaired skeep for scaring away birds
34 A weiphing windscreen
35 A klarting abacus
36 A lely picture frame to replace a standard parachute
37 A mursing crossword puzzle
38 A fleirdly cake kept under a child's bed
39 A perfectly spherical stourve for heating a cold house
40 A wrierh with which to splooh a glopp
41 A kraecrly lioness to show that you care
42 The remains of a gargantuan brirm
43 A nourping calendar
44 A traeping mourk
45 A paesing cockatoo
46 A sclerily pig for attaching to a bike
47 A siring picture
48 A skliany world map which has been sandpapered smooth
49 A phaiz with which to phokle a quurn
50 A hoorcly briasp
51 A flying blooph with a broken top
52 A gilded skoum for use in cooking
53 A fast sheeple to assist with company mergers
54 A briling post it note
55 A gruply telephone answering machine
56 A cucrly scrooj

57	A smelly bliarg decorated with beads	59	A wiabing scluny
58	A perfectly spherical deiple	60	An Australian poudy displayed on a postage stamp

5.19 Shades

Feel free to invent your own adjectives, but this list will give you a prompt if you need some in a hurry. Don't try to select an adjective to fit the problem, pick one at random. The list has 60 words to facilitate the method popularized by Edward de Bono of choosing an item by checking the second hand of a watch.

1	Pink	36	Lustrous
2	Purple	37	Shiny
3	Red	38	See-through
4	Green	39	Loud
5	Yellow	40	Quiet
6	Blue	41	Harmonious
7	Brown	42	Squeaky
8	Orange	43	Bulging
9	Turquoise	44	Wooden
10	Black	45	Plastic
11	White	46	Metallic
12	Fluffy	47	Flexible
13	Furry	48	Rigid
14	Hard	49	Patient
15	Scratchy	50	Caring
16	Bubbly	51	Nosy
17	Explosive	52	Greedy
18	Sharp	53	Motherly
19	Smooth	54	Angry
20	Oily	55	Happy
21	Slimy	56	Naughty
22	Hot	57	Enormous
23	Cold	58	Tiny
24	Icy	59	Fat
25	Limp	60	Thin
26	Pungent		
27	Rancid		
28	Delicious		
29	Sweet		
30	Sour		
31	Salty		
32	Acidic		
33	Electrifying		
34	Thrusting		
35	Sexy		